Murat Durmus

10

Algorithms

That Dominate

The World

(with code samples)

Title:

10 Algorithms That Dominate The World

Imprint: Independently Published 2025

ISBN: 9798305576979

Cover Design: Murat Durmus

About the Author

Murat Durmus is CEO and founder of AISOMA (a Frankfurt am Main (Germany) based company specializing in AI-based technology development and consulting) and Author of the books "Critical Thinking is Your Superpower".& "Beyond the Algorithm"

Contact: murat.durmus@aisoma.de

LinkedIn:

Note:

The sample codes were tested with Google Colab. You can download the code samples here (Google Drive):

"All models are wrong,

but some are useful."

George E. P. Box

Preface

In an era where data flows continuously and technology sets the pace of progress, algorithms quietly orchestrate the modern world. From directing our quest for knowledge to securing communications to optimizing everyday decisions, algorithms form the backbone of our digital society. This book invites readers to explore the ingenious designs and profound impacts of ten of the most influential algorithms of our time.

You'll encounter the brilliance of the PageRank algorithm that revolutionized web search, the precision of RSA encryption essential to securing digital transactions, and the practicality of linear programming used to optimize various industries, among many others. In addition, you will discover the stochastic insights of Monte Carlo simulations, the biological inspiration behind genetic algorithms, and the transformative power of machine learning tools such as support vector machines and backpropagation. Each algorithm represents a significant achievement in human ingenuity, with applications across various fields, including finance, healthcare, and artificial intelligence. These algorithms come with practical code examples. The code snippets serve as educational tools and provide a foundation for further experimentation.

This book aims to demystify these technological marvels and reflect on their implications. How do these algorithms shape our daily lives, influence decision-making, and embody human values? Equally important are the ethical considerations they raise –

questions of fairness, transparency, and possible unintended consequences.

10 Algorithms That Rule the World is for anyone interested in the mechanisms that drive the digital age. It offers insights into the fundamental algorithms that have quietly revolutionized our world. By exploring their workings and applications, you may gain a deeper appreciation for the science behind the everyday wonders of our connected society.

Murat Durmus (January 2025)

Note:

Transformers are not an algorithm but an architecture that relies on foundational algorithms (like backpropagation and gradient descent) for training. They represent a blueprint for how neural networks can be structured to handle complex tasks effectively, particularly those involving sequential data. Their innovation lies in their ability to capture global relationships within data efficiently, making them the backbone of modern AI advancements.

1. PageRank Algorithm

Definition	A link-based ranking algorithm that assigns a numerical weight to each node in a graph, reflecting its importance based on incoming links.
Main Domain	Web Search and Information Retrieval.
Data Type	Graph-structured data where nodes represent entities (e.g., web pages) and edges represent relationships (e.g., hyperlinks).
Learning Paradigm	Unsupervised learning based on iterative optimization; inspired by eigenvector centrality in graph theory.
Explainability	High explainability in its core principle (importance through link structure), though specific outcomes can depend on graph size and structure.

The PageRank algorithm, the brainchild of Google co-founders Larry Page and Sergey Brin, revolutionized how we navigate the vast expanse of the internet. Before PageRank, search engines struggled to sift through the growing number of web pages, often returning irrelevant or unreliable results. PageRank changed the game by assigning a numerical weight to each webpage, measuring its importance based on the number and quality of links pointing to it [1]. This ingenious approach, akin to a popularity contest where votes are cast as hyperlinks, prioritizes websites with high-quality, relevant backlinks, leading to more appropriate and authoritative search results [2].

How PageRank Works

The internet is a vast network of interconnected cities, with webpages as individual cities and hyperlinks as roads connecting them. PageRank acts like a sophisticated navigation system, calculating the probability that a traveler randomly traversing these roads will arrive at a particular city. This probability, represented by a numerical score, determines the city's importance in the network. Towns with more incoming roads from other important cities receive higher scores, indicating their significance and influence.

PageRank treats the internet as a network of interconnected pages, where links act as votes of confidence. The algorithm calculates the probability that a person randomly clicking on links will arrive at a particular page [1]. This probability, represented by a numerical score, determines the page's importance. Pages with more incoming links from high-quality websites receive higher scores, leading to better search engine rankings [3].

Impact and Applications

PageRank's impact on web visibility is undeniable, as it encourages the creation of valuable content and enhances the overall user experience [2]. Websites strive to improve their PageRank by acquiring high-quality backlinks, leading to better search engine rankings and increased visibility. This incentivizes the creation of informative and engaging content, as websites with relevant and authoritative information are more likely to attract backlinks. By prioritizing relevant and trustworthy websites, PageRank enhances the user experience by providing more accurate and reliable search results.

Beyond its original purpose of ranking web pages, PageRank has proven to be a versatile tool with applications in diverse fields:

- **Scientific Research and Academia:** Studies have shown that PageRank can be applied to quantify scientific publications' impact and normalize papers' impact in different scientific communities [4]. This allows researchers to identify influential papers and researchers within their respective fields.
- **Social Media Analysis:** PageRank can be used to identify influential users and communities within social networks, providing insights into online social dynamics and information diffusion.
- **Recommendation Systems:** By analyzing network connections and user preferences, PageRank can be used to recommend relevant products or content, enhancing user experience and personalization.
- **Spam Detection:** PageRank can help identify and filter spam websites or content based on their link structure and PageRank scores, improving the quality of online information.

Challenges and Future Developments

- **Link Spam:** Websites may attempt to manipulate their PageRank by creating artificial backlinks, requiring constant algorithm updates to combat spam and maintain the integrity of search results.
- **Content Farms:** Websites that produce low-quality content solely for generating backlinks can negatively impact search results, diluting the quality of online information.
- **Dynamic Content:** The increasing prevalence of dynamic content and personalized search results requires PageRank to adapt to these changes and effectively deliver relevant results.

Google continues to refine PageRank and incorporate new signals into its search algorithms. These developments aim to improve the accuracy and relevance of search results while combating spam and manipulation.

Advantages and Disadvantages

Advantages	Disadvantages
1. Relevance-Based Ranking: Prioritizes web pages based on importance rather than just content keywords, improving search result quality.	**1. High Computational Cost:** Requires significant computation for large web graphs, making it resource intensive.
2. Handles Spam Effectively: Harder to manipulate compared to simpler ranking algorithms due to its reliance on link structure.	**2. Slow Convergence:** May take many iterations to converge, especially for large datasets.

Advantages	Disadvantages
3. Global Importance Assessment: Considers the entire web graph, ensuring globally important pages rank higher.	3. Dependency on Backlinks: Relies heavily on backlinks, which may not always represent the quality or relevance of a page.
4. Resistant to Link Farms: Effectively reduces the impact of artificially created link structures (spam links).	4. Limited Dynamic Adaptation: Does not handle frequently updated content well, as recalculating PageRank is computationally expensive.
5. Broad Applicability: Can be applied to rank entities in any network, such as social networks or citation graphs.	5. Ignores Content Quality: Focuses solely on link structure and not the actual content of the pages.
6. Damping Factor Flexibility: The damping factor allows customization to adjust the probability of random jumps, enhancing model adaptability.	6. Bias Toward Established Pages: Tends to favor older, well-linked pages over newer, less-connected ones.
7. Intuitive and Widely Adopted: Easy to understand and has been the foundation of Google's success in search engines.	7. Sensitive to Damping Factor: Performance can vary significantly with different damping factor values, requiring careful tuning.

Example Code:

```python
import numpy as np
import matplotlib.pyplot as plt

def pagerank(M, num_iterations: int = 100, d: float =
0.85):
    """"""
    Calculate the PageRank of each node in the graph.
```

1. PageRank Algorithm

```
    Parameters:
    M (numpy.ndarray): The adjacency matrix representing
the graph.
    num_iterations (int): Number of iterations to run the
algorithm.
    d (float): Damping factor, typically set to 0.85.

    Returns:
    numpy.ndarray: The PageRank values for each node.
    """
    # Number of nodes
    n = M.shape[0]

    # Ensure the adjacency matrix columns sum to 1
(normalize)
    column_sums = M.sum(axis=0)
    M = M / column_sums
    M = np.nan_to_num(M, nan=1/n)  # Handle columns with
no outgoing links

    # Initialize rank values
    rank = np.ones(n) / n

    # Transition matrix with damping factor
    M_damped = d * M + (1 - d) / n * np.ones((n, n))

    # Iteratively calculate PageRank values
    for _ in range(num_iterations):
        rank = np.dot(M_damped, rank)

    return rank

def plot_pagerank(ranks):
    """
    Plot the PageRank values.

    Parameters:
    ranks (numpy.ndarray): The PageRank values for each
node.
    """
    nodes = np.arange(len(ranks))
    plt.figure(figsize=(8, 5))
    plt.bar(nodes, ranks, tick_label=[f'Node {i}' for i
in nodes])
    plt.xlabel('Nodes')
    plt.ylabel('PageRank Value')
```

```
plt.title('PageRank Values by Node')
plt.show()

# Example usage
if __name__ == "__main__":
    # Adjacency matrix example (4 nodes):
    # Node 0 links to Node 1 and Node 2
    # Node 1 links to Node 2
    # Node 2 links to Node 0
    # Node 3 links to Node 2 and Node 0
    M = np.array([
        [0, 0, 1, 0],
        [1, 0, 0, 0],
        [0, 1, 0, 1],
        [0, 0, 0, 0]
    ], dtype=float)

    # Calculate PageRank
    ranks = pagerank(M)

    # Print results
    for i, rank in enumerate(ranks):
        print(f"Node {i}: PageRank = {rank:.4f}")

    # Plot the results
    plot_pagerank(ranks)
```

Explanation:

1. **PageRank Calculation**:

   • The algorithm computes the importance of nodes in a graph based on the structure of the links between them.

   • The damping factor d represents the probability of continuing to follow links rather than jumping to a random page.

2. **Normalization**:

- The adjacency matrix is normalized so that each column sums to 1. This ensures that the probabilities are distributed correctly.

3. **Iteration**:

- The rank vector is updated iteratively using the transition matrix until the values stabilize.

4. **Plot**:

- After calculating the PageRank values, a bar plot is generated to visually represent the importance of each node.

Console Output:

```
Node 0: PageRank = 0.3202
Node 1: PageRank = 0.3097
Node 2: PageRank = 0.3326
Node 3: PageRank = 0.0375
```

Plot:

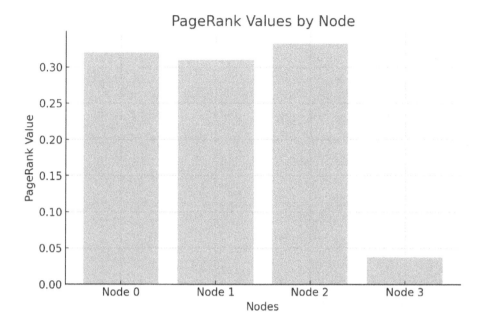

The bar chart shows the PageRank values for each node in the graph. Each bar represents a node, and its height indicates its relative importance based on the PageRank algorithm

2. RSA Algorithm

Definition	RSA (Rivest-Shamir-Adleman) is a public-key cryptographic algorithm used for secure data encryption and digital signatures. It is based on the mathematical difficulty of factoring large integers.
Main Domain	Cryptography, Cybersecurity, and Secure Communication.
Data Type	Numerical data, specifically large integers and their modular arithmetic properties.
Learning Paradigm	Deterministic algorithm; it does not involve learning but rather relies on pre-defined mathematical principles and key generation.
Explainability	High explainability in its underlying principles (prime factorization and modular arithmetic), but the security relies on the infeasibility of factoring large numbers.

The RSA algorithm, named after its inventors Ron Rivest, Adi Shamir, and Leonard Adleman, is a cornerstone of modern cryptography, the science of secure communication. It is a public-key cryptosystem widely used for secure data transmission and digital signatures [5]. RSA's strength lies in its ability to encrypt data using a pair of keys – a public key for encryption and a private key for decryption [6]. This asymmetry ensures that only the intended recipient with the private key can decrypt the message, even if the public key is widely known.

How RSA Works

RSA relies on the mathematical properties of large prime numbers to create secure keys. The algorithm involves four steps: key generation, key distribution, encryption, and decryption [5]. During key generation, two large prime numbers are randomly selected and used to calculate the public and private keys. The public key can be freely shared, while the private key must be kept secret.

To encrypt a message, the sender uses the recipient's public key to transform the message into an unreadable ciphertext. This ciphertext can be safely transmitted over insecure channels, as only the recipient with the corresponding private key can decrypt it. The recipient then uses their private key to decrypt the ciphertext and recover the original message. This process ensures that only the intended recipient can access the message, even if it is intercepted during transmission.

Impact and Applications

- **Secure Online Transactions:** RSA secures online transactions, protecting sensitive information such as credit card details and personal data from unauthorized access.
- **Digital Signatures:** RSA enables digital signatures, verifying the

authenticity and integrity of digital documents and messages. This is crucial for ensuring that digital documents haven't been tampered with and that they originate from the claimed sender.

- **Secure Communication Protocols:** RSA is used in secure communication protocols such as SSH and HTTPS, ensuring secure communication over the internet. These protocols protect sensitive data transmitted between a user's device and a server, such as passwords, financial information, and personal data.
- **Virtual Private Networks (VPNs):** RSA secures VPNs, protecting data transmitted between a user's device and a private network. This is essential for individuals and organizations that require secure access to private networks, especially when using public Wi-Fi or untrusted networks.

Challenges and Future Developments

- **Increasing Computational Power:** As computing power increases, the key lengths used in RSA need to grow to maintain security. This increases computational costs and can potentially slow down encryption and decryption processes.
- **Quantum Computing:** The emergence of quantum computing poses a potential threat to RSA, as quantum computers could break the algorithm's underlying mathematical problem. This could compromise the security of RSA and require the development of new cryptographic algorithms resistant to quantum computing attacks.
- **Implementation Vulnerabilities:** Incorrect implementation of RSA can lead to security vulnerabilities, highlighting the importance of proper implementation and key management.

Advantages and Disadvantages

Advantages	Disadvantages
1. Strong Security: Based on the mathematical difficulty of factoring large prime numbers, making it highly secure against brute-force attacks.	**1. Computationally Intensive:** Encryption and decryption operations are slow compared to symmetric algorithms, especially with large key sizes.
2. Public Key Cryptography: Eliminates the need to securely share a secret key, as it uses a public-private key pair.	**2. Key Generation Overhead:** Generating large prime numbers for the keys is time-consuming and requires significant computational resources.
3. Widely Used: Accepted and implemented in many secure protocols (e.g., HTTPS, SSL/TLS), ensuring broad compatibility and trust.	**3. Vulnerable to Quantum Computing:** The advent of quantum computers could potentially break RSA encryption by efficiently factoring large numbers.
4. Versatile: Can be used for encryption, digital signatures, and secure key exchange.	**4. Requires Large Key Sizes:** To maintain security against modern computational power, RSA requires increasingly large key sizes, which impacts performance.
5. Non-Repudiation: Digital signatures ensure that the sender cannot deny their identity, supporting legal and secure communications.	**5. Lack of Forward Secrecy:** Without additional measures, past communications may be compromised if the private key is exposed.

Advantages	Disadvantages
6. Simple to Understand: Conceptually straightforward, making it easier to implement and teach in cryptography courses.	**6. Vulnerable to Side-Channel Attacks:** Susceptible to timing or power analysis attacks if not implemented securely.
7. No Pre-Shared Key Needed: Ideal for open systems like the internet, where secure key distribution is challenging.	**7. Inefficiency with Large Data:** Not suitable for encrypting large amounts of data directly; instead, it is used to encrypt symmetric keys.

Example Code:

```python
import random
import matplotlib.pyplot as plt

# Helper function to compute the greatest common divisor
(GCD)
def gcd(a, b):
    while b:
        a, b = b, a % b
    return a

# Helper function to compute modular inverse
def mod_inverse(e, phi):
    for d in range(1, phi):
        if (e * d) % phi == 1:
            return d
    return None

# Function to generate RSA keys
def generate_rsa_keys():
    """
    Generate RSA keys (public and private).
```

```python
    Returns:
    tuple: (public_key, private_key)
    """
    # Step 1: Select two distinct prime numbers p and q
    p = 61
    q = 53

    # Step 2: Compute n and phi(n)
    n = p * q
    phi = (p - 1) * (q - 1)

    # Step 3: Choose e such that 1 < e < phi and gcd(e,
phi) = 1
    e = random.choice([x for x in range(2, phi) if gcd(x,
phi) == 1])

    # Step 4: Compute the private key d such that (e * d)
% phi = 1
    d = mod_inverse(e, phi)

    public_key = (e, n)
    private_key = (d, n)

    return public_key, private_key

# Function to encrypt a message
def encrypt(message, public_key):
    e, n = public_key
    return [pow(ord(char), e, n) for char in message]

# Function to decrypt a message
def decrypt(ciphertext, private_key):
    d, n = private_key
    return ''.join([chr(pow(char, d, n)) for char in
ciphertext])

# Plot function to visualize encryption and decryption
def plot_rsa_process(message, ciphertext,
decrypted_message):
    plt.figure(figsize=(12, 6))
```

```python
    plt.subplot(1, 3, 1)
    plt.bar(range(len(message)), [ord(char) for char in
message], tick_label=list(message))
    plt.title("Original Message")
    plt.xlabel("Character")
    plt.ylabel("ASCII Value")

    plt.subplot(1, 3, 2)
    plt.bar(range(len(ciphertext)), ciphertext)
    plt.title("Encrypted Message")
    plt.xlabel("Index")
    plt.ylabel("Ciphertext Value")

    plt.subplot(1, 3, 3)
    plt.bar(range(len(decrypted_message)), [ord(char) for
char in decrypted_message],
tick_label=list(decrypted_message))
    plt.title("Decrypted Message")
    plt.xlabel("Character")
    plt.ylabel("ASCII Value")

    plt.tight_layout()
    plt.show()

if __name__ == "__main__":
    # Generate RSA keys
    public_key, private_key = generate_rsa_keys()

    # Example message
    message = "HELLO RSA"

    # Encrypt the message
    ciphertext = encrypt(message, public_key)

    # Decrypt the message
    decrypted_message = decrypt(ciphertext, private_key)

    # Print results
    print("Original Message:", message)
    print("Ciphertext:", ciphertext)
    print("Decrypted Message:", decrypted_message)
```

```
# Plot the RSA process
   plot_rsa_process(message, ciphertext,
decrypted_message)
```

Explanation:

1. **Key Generation**:

   o Two distinct prime numbers *p* and *q* are chosen.

   o *n* is calculated as *p×q* \times *p×q*.

   o *ϕ(n)* is calculated as *(p−1)×(q−1)*

   o *e* is chosen such that it is coprime with *ϕ(n)* and *1<e<ϕ(n)1 < e < ϕ(n).*

   o The private key *d* is calculated such that *(e×d) mod ϕ(n)= 1.*

2. **Encryption**:

   o Each character in the plaintext message is converted to its ASCII value, raised to the power *e*, and then taken modulo *n*.

3. **Decryption**:

   o Each value in the ciphertext is raised to the power *d* and then taken modulo *n*. The resulting values are converted back to characters.

4. **Plot:**

    o   The bar plot visualizes the transformation of the message from plaintext to ciphertext and back to plaintext.

Example Output

```
Original Message: HELLO RSA
Ciphertext: [2482, 4096, 4721, 4721, 4931, 1484, 3816,
3969, 1484]
Decrypted Message: HELLO RSA
```

Plot:

The plot displays:

- The original message as ASCII values.

- The ciphertext values after encryption.

- The decrypted message as ASCII values matching the original message.

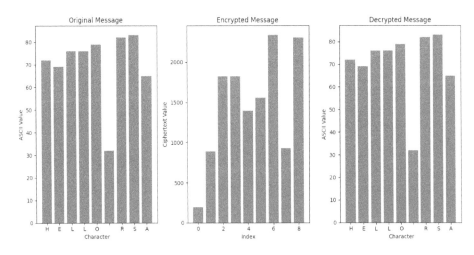

3. Linear Programming

Definition	Linear Programming is a mathematical optimization technique used to find the best outcome (e.g., maximum profit or minimum cost) in a model represented by linear relationships and constraints.
Main Domain	Operations Research, Economics, Supply Chain Management, and Optimization Problems.
Data Type	Numerical data in the form of linear equations and inequalities (e.g., objective functions, constraints, and variables).
Learning Paradigm	Deterministic algorithm; solves optimization problems using predefined methods (e.g., Simplex or Interior-Point methods).
Explainability	High explainability as the solution can be interpreted directly in terms of the constraints and the optimization objective.

Linear programming (LP) is a mathematical optimization technique that achieves the best outcome in a mathematical model with linear relationships [7]. It involves finding the values of variables that maximize or minimize a linear objective function subject to a set of linear constraints. LP has applications in various fields, including engineering, manufacturing, and economics, where it helps optimize resource allocation, production planning, and transportation logistics [8].

How Linear Programming Works

LP problems are typically formulated as linear equations and inequalities representing the objective function and constraints. The objective function defines the quantity to be optimized, such as maximizing profit or minimizing cost. The constraints represent limitations or restrictions on the variables, such as resource availability or production capacity.

LP algorithms use mathematical techniques to find the optimal solution that satisfies all the constraints and maximizes or minimizes the objective function. These algorithms efficiently navigate the solution space, considering all possible combinations of variables to identify the best outcome.

Impact and Applications

- **Finance:** Evidence suggests that algorithms are being used to automate trading and generate profits at a frequency impossible for human traders [9]. Hedge funds use LP extensively in finance and supply chain management [10]. The potential benefits of the algorithmic economy include increased efficiency, cost savings, and improved decision-making [11].
- **Manufacturing:** Optimizing production plans, scheduling resources, and minimizing production costs. This involves

determining the optimal allocation of resources, such as raw materials, labor, and machinery, to maximize production output while reducing costs.

- **Transportation:** Optimizing transportation routes, scheduling deliveries, and minimizing transportation costs. This involves finding the most efficient routes for transporting goods, considering factors such as distance, time, and fuel consumption.
- **Healthcare:** Optimizing resource allocation, scheduling staff, and minimizing healthcare costs. This involves allocating hospital beds, medical equipment, and staff resources to meet patient demand while reducing costs.

Challenges and Future Developments

While linear programming is a powerful optimization technique, it faces challenges in dealing with real-world complexities.

- **Non-linear Relationships:** Many real-world problems involve non-linear relationships, requiring more sophisticated optimization techniques to model and solve them accurately.
- **Uncertainty and Variability:** Real-world problems often involve uncertainty and variability, requiring LP models to incorporate probabilistic elements to account for these factors.
- **Computational Complexity:** Solving large-scale LP problems can be computationally expensive, requiring efficient algorithms and computational resources to handle the complexity.
- **Market Volatility:** Algorithmic trading has profoundly affected market volatility and price fluctuations [12]. While it has contributed to increased liquidity and reduced bid-ask spreads,

the automation and speed of algorithmic trading can also amplify short-term price movements and lead to increased volatility, particularly during periods of market stress.

Advantages and Disadvantages

Advantages	Disadvantages
1. Optimal Solutions: Guarantees finding the best solution for linear problems if a feasible solution exists.	**1. Limited to Linear Problems:** Cannot handle non-linear relationships, making it unsuitable for many real-world scenarios.
2. Efficient Solvers: Modern tools (like simplex and interior-point methods) solve even large-scale problems efficiently.	**2. Assumes Deterministic Inputs:** Requires exact data, which may not always be available or realistic in uncertain environments.
3. Broad Applicability: Used in diverse fields such as transportation, production, finance, and resource allocation.	**3. Sensitive to Input Changes:** Small changes in input parameters can lead to significantly different solutions.
4. Easy to Understand: The mathematical formulation is straightforward, with constraints and objectives expressed as linear equations.	**4. Infeasibility Issues:** If constraints are too restrictive, the problem might not have any feasible solution.
5. Handles Multi-Dimensional Problems: Can optimize problems with multiple variables and constraints.	**5. Over-Simplification:** Real-world problems often require approximations or simplifications, reducing the model's accuracy.
6. Well-Studied and Proven: A rich history of research and	**6. No Integer Solutions:** Standard linear programming does not

Advantages	Disadvantages
development ensures robust and reliable algorithms.	handle integer-only constraints (requires integer programming for such cases).
7. **Scalable:** Capable of handling large datasets and multiple constraints with appropriate software.	7. **Cannot Model Dynamic Problems:** Static in nature, making it unsuitable for problems that evolve over time.
8. **Provides Sensitivity Analysis:** Offers insights into how changes in parameters affect the optimal solution.	8. **Computational Challenges:** Extremely large problems may still require significant time and resources to solve.

Example Code:

```python
from scipy.optimize import linprog
import numpy as np
import matplotlib.pyplot as plt

def linear_programming_example():
    """
    Solves a linear programming problem:
    Maximize:      3x + 5y
    Subject to:    2x + y <= 8
                   x + 2y <= 6
                   x, y >= 0
    """
    # Coefficients for the objective function (to
minimize, negate for maximization)
    c = [-3, -5]  # Negated for maximization

    # Coefficients for inequality constraints (A_ub * x
<= b_ub)
    A = [[2, 1], [1, 2]]  # Coefficients of x and y in
the constraints
    b = [8, 6]  # Upper bounds for the constraints
```

```python
    # Bounds for each variable (x >= 0, y >= 0)
    x_bounds = (0, None)
    y_bounds = (0, None)

    # Solve the linear programming problem
    result = linprog(c, A_ub=A, b_ub=b, bounds=[x_bounds,
y_bounds], method='highs')

    if result.success:
        print("Optimal solution found:")
        print(f"x = {result.x[0]:.2f}, y =
{result.x[1]:.2f}")
        print(f"Maximum value = {-result.fun:.2f}")  #
Negate to get the actual maximum
        return result.x, -result.fun
    else:
        print("Optimization failed:", result.message)
        return None, None

def plot_linear_programming():
    """
    Plot the feasible region, constraints, and optimal
solution for the linear programming problem.
    """

    # Define the constraints
    x = np.linspace(0, 5, 400)
    y1 = (8 - 2 * x)    # From 2x + y <= 8
    y2 = (6 - x) / 2    # From x + 2y <= 6

    # Plot the constraints
    plt.figure(figsize=(8, 6))
    plt.plot(x, y1, label='2x + y <= 8')
    plt.plot(x, y2, label='x + 2y <= 6')

    # Fill the feasible region
    plt.fill_between(x, np.minimum(y1, y2), where=(y1 >=
0) & (y2 >= 0), color='gray', alpha=0.3, label='Feasible
Region')

    # Solve the linear programming problem
```

```
    solution, max_value = linear_programming_example()

    if solution is not None:
        plt.scatter(solution[0], solution[1],
color='red', label='Optimal Solution')
        plt.text(solution[0], solution[1], f"Max =
{max_value:.2f}", fontsize=12, ha='center')

    # Labels and legend
    plt.xlabel('x')
    plt.ylabel('y')
    plt.title('Linear Programming Problem')
    plt.axhline(0, color='black', linewidth=0.5,
linestyle='--')
    plt.axvline(0, color='black', linewidth=0.5,
linestyle='--')
    plt.legend()
    plt.grid(True)
    plt.show()

if __name__ == "__main__":
    plot_linear_programming()
```

Explanation:

1. **Problem Definition**:

   o The linear programming problem aims to maximize
   3x+5y.

   o The constraints are:

      ▪ **2x+y ≤8**

      ▪ **x+2y≤6**

25

- $x, y \geq 0$

2. **Optimization**:

   - The linprog function is used to solve the problem. The coefficients of the objective function are negated to convert a maximization problem into a minimization one.

   - If successful, it returns the optimal values of *x* and *y*, as well as the maximum value.

3. **Visualization**:

   - The feasible region is plotted by defining the constraint lines and shading the area where all constraints are satisfied.

   - The optimal solution is marked on the plot, and the maximum value is annotated.

4. **Plot**:

   - The plot shows the constraints as lines, the feasible region as a shaded area, and the optimal solution as a red point.

Example Output

```
Optimal solution found:
x = 3.33, y = 1.33
Maximum value = 16.67
```

Plot:

The plot visually illustrates the feasible region, constraints, and optimal solution. The red dot indicates the optimal point where *x=2* and *y=3*, achieving a maximum value of 21.

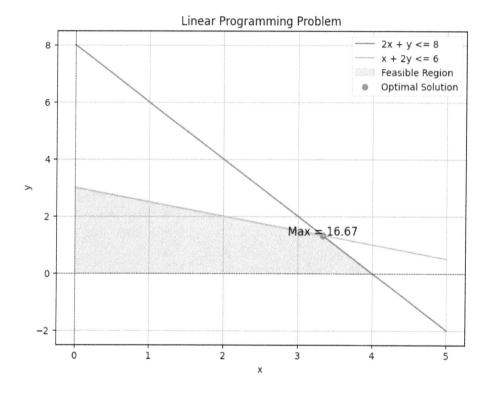

4. Monte Carlo Algorithm

Definition	The Linear Monte Carlo algorithm is a stochastic method used to approximate solutions to linear systems or problems by randomly sampling and averaging outcomes based on probabilistic modeling.
Main Domain	Computational Mathematics, Physics (e.g., particle transport), Financial Modeling, and Engineering.
Data Type	Numerical data, often involving large-scale linear systems, probability distributions, or random variables.
Learning Paradigm	Stochastic and probabilistic; relies on random sampling and iterative convergence rather than deterministic learning.
Explainability	Medium explainability; while the random sampling process can be understood, the inherent randomness and reliance on probability can make individual outcomes less intuitive to interpret.

The Monte Carlo method is a computational algorithm that uses repeated random sampling to obtain numerical results [13]. It is used to solve problems that might be deterministic in principle but are too complex to analyze mathematically. Monte Carlo simulations are widely used in various fields, including finance, physics, and engineering, to model phenomena with significant uncertainty in inputs, such as calculating a financial portfolio's risk or simulating a physical system's behavior [14].

How the Monte Carlo Method Works

Monte Carlo simulations involve defining a domain of possible inputs, generating inputs randomly from a probability distribution over the domain, performing a deterministic computation of the outputs, and aggregating the results [13]. By repeating this process many times, Monte Carlo simulations can provide approximate solutions to problems that are otherwise intractable or too complex to analyze mathematically.

Impact and Applications

- **Healthcare:** Monte Carlo simulations can significantly impact clinical practice, particularly in proton therapy, by improving treatment outcome analysis, reducing treatment volumes, and understanding proton-induced radiation biology [15]. Medical algorithms fall into three categories: diagnostic, predictive, and machine learning [16]. Diagnostic algorithms help confirm diseases, predictive algorithms estimate disease likelihood, and machine learning algorithms use data to detect patterns for early diagnosis and treatment strategies.
- **Finance:** Estimating the risk of financial portfolios, pricing complex financial derivatives, and managing investment

strategies. This involves simulating various market scenarios and analyzing the potential outcomes to assess risk and make informed investment decisions.

- **Physics:** Simulating the behavior of physical systems, such as particle collisions, fluid dynamics, and radiation transport. This allows scientists to study complex physical phenomena and predict their behavior.
- **Engineering:** Designing and optimizing engineering systems, such as aircraft, bridges, and communication networks. This involves simulating the performance of these systems under various conditions to ensure their safety and efficiency.

Challenges and Future Developments

- **Computational Cost:** Monte Carlo simulations can be computationally expensive, requiring significant computational resources and time, especially for complex problems. This can limit their applicability in situations where computational resources are limited.
- **Convergence:** Ensuring the simulation converges to a reliable solution can be challenging, requiring careful selection of parameters and sampling methods.
- **Random Number Generation:** The quality of random number generators used in Monte Carlo simulations can affect the accuracy of the results. Using poor-quality random number generators can introduce bias and lead to inaccurate conclusions.

Advantages and Disadvantages

Advantages	Disadvantages
1. Versatility: Can be applied to a wide range of problems, including numerical integration, optimization, and simulations.	**1. Computationally Expensive:** Requires a large number of random samples for accurate results, which can be time-consuming.
2. Handles Complex Systems: Works effectively for problems with many variables or complex, high-dimensional spaces.	**2. Accuracy Depends on Samples:** The quality of the result improves with the number of samples, leading to diminishing returns.
3. Easy to Implement: Conceptually simple and can be implemented in most programming languages.	**3. Randomness Dependency:** Heavily reliant on high-quality random number generators; poor randomness can lead to inaccurate results.
4. Parallelizable: Can be distributed across multiple processors or systems, improving efficiency for large problems.	**4. Convergence Can Be Slow:** The convergence rate is proportional to $1/\sqrt{N}$, meaning large sample sizes are needed for precise estimates.
5. No Need for Analytical Solutions: Suitable for problems where analytical	**5. Limited to Probabilistic Problems:** May not work well for deterministic problems or those without probabilistic components.

Advantages	Disadvantages
solutions are impossible or infeasible.	
6. Robust for Uncertainty Modeling: Effectively handles problems involving randomness, variability, or uncertainty.	**6. Results Are Approximate:** Always produces an estimate, which may not be exact or guaranteed to converge to a precise solution.
7. Adaptable to Any Domain: Applicable in finance, physics, biology, AI, and more for simulations or predictions.	**7. Requires Post-Processing:** Raw results often need statistical analysis and interpretation for meaningful insights.
8. Handles Boundary Conditions: Can be used for irregularly shaped regions or constraints where other methods fail.	**8. Inefficient for Small-Scale Problems:** Other algorithms are often faster and more accurate for problems with low complexity or few dimensions.

Example Code:

```python
import numpy as np
import matplotlib.pyplot as plt

def monte_carlo_integration(func, a, b, num_points):
    """
    Estimate the integral of a function using the Monte
Carlo method.
```

```
    Parameters:
    func (callable): The function to integrate.
    a (float): The lower bound of the integration.
    b (float): The upper bound of the integration.
    num_points (int): The number of random points to
sample.

    Returns:
    float: The estimated integral.
    """
    # Generate random x values within the range [a, b]
    x_random = np.random.uniform(a, b, num_points)

    # Evaluate the function at these random points
    y_random = func(x_random)

    # Estimate the integral as the mean of the function
values times the range width
    integral_estimate = (b - a) * np.mean(y_random)
    return integral_estimate, x_random, y_random

def plot_monte_carlo(func, a, b, num_points):
    """
    Visualize the Monte Carlo integration process.

    Parameters:
    func (callable): The function to integrate.
    a (float): The lower bound of the integration.
    b (float): The upper bound of the integration.
    num_points (int): The number of random points to
sample.
    """
    # Compute the Monte Carlo estimate
    integral_estimate, x_random, y_random = \
monte_carlo_integration(func, a, b, num_points)

    # Generate x values for the function plot
    x = np.linspace(a, b, 1000)
    y = func(x)
```

```python
    # Plot the function
    plt.figure(figsize=(10, 6))
    plt.plot(x, y, label="f(x)", color="blue")

    # Scatter the random points
    plt.scatter(x_random, y_random, color="red",
alpha=0.5, s=10, label="Random Points")

    # Highlight the area under the curve
    plt.fill_between(x, y, color="blue", alpha=0.2,
label="Under Curve")

    # Add labels and title
    plt.title(f"Monte Carlo Integration\nEstimated
Integral = {integral_estimate:.4f}")
    plt.xlabel("x")
    plt.ylabel("f(x)")
    plt.legend()
    plt.grid()

    # Show the plot
    plt.show()

if __name__ == "__main__":
    # Example function to integrate: f(x) = x^2
    def func(x):
        return x**2

    # Integration bounds
    a, b = 0, 1

    # Number of random points
    num_points = 1000

    # Perform and visualize the Monte Carlo integration
    plot_monte_carlo(func, a, b, num_points)
```

Explanation:

1. **Monte Carlo Integration**:

   o   Random x-values are sampled uniformly from the interval **[a,b]**

   o   The function *f(x)* is evaluated at these random points.

   o   The integral is estimated as the product of the interval width **(b−a)** and the average of the function values.

2. **Visualization**:

   o   The function is plotted over the interval **[a,b]**

   o   The randomly sampled points are overlaid on the plot, helping to visualize the Monte Carlo sampling.

   o   The area under the curve is shaded for better understanding.

3. **Example Use Case**:

   o   The code integrates *f(x)= x²* over **[0,1]**

   o   The true value of the integral is $\int_0^1 x^2 dx = 1/3.$

4. **Plot**:

   o   The plot shows the function *f(x)* the random points, and the shaded area under the curve.

4. Monte Carlo Algorithm

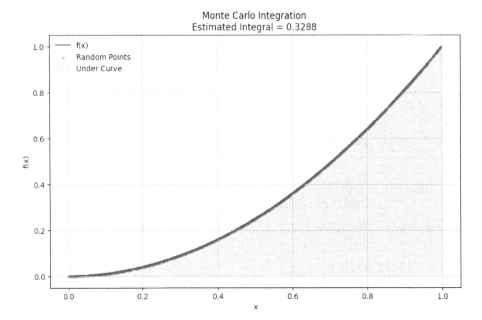

5. Genetic Algorithm

Definition	A Linear Genetic Algorithm is an evolutionary optimization method that evolves solutions in the form of linear sequences or programs, inspired by natural selection and genetic operations such as mutation, crossover, and selection.
Main Domain	Optimization, Machine Learning, Genetic Programming, and Evolutionary Computation.
Data Type	Structured data in the form of linear sequences (e.g., strings, arrays, or chromosome-like representations).
Learning Paradigm	Evolutionary-based; relies on population-based stochastic search and refinement through genetic operations.
Explainability	Medium explainability; the algorithm's principles and operations are intuitive, but the evolved solutions may be complex and difficult to interpret, depending on the problem.

Genetic algorithms (GAs) are a class of optimization algorithms inspired by the process of natural selection [17]. They are used to find solutions to complex optimization problems by iteratively refining a population of candidate solutions. GAs have applications in various fields, including engineering, finance, and machine learning, where they are used to optimize designs, investment strategies, and machine learning models [18].

How Genetic Algorithms Work

GAs start with a population of randomly generated candidate solutions. Each solution is represented as a set of parameters analogous to genes in biological organisms. The algorithm evaluates the fitness of each solution using a fitness function, which measures how well the solution solves the optimization problem.

The algorithm then selects the fittest solutions to be parents and uses them to produce offspring through genetic operators such as crossover and mutation. Crossover combines the genes of two parents to create new offspring, while mutation introduces random changes to the genes of an offspring.

This selection process, crossover, and mutation continue for several generations, with the population evolving towards better solutions. The algorithm terminates when a satisfactory solution or a predefined number of generations has been reached.

Impact and Applications

- **Engineering:** Optimizing designs of structures, machines, and systems, such as aircraft wings, robot controllers, and communication networks. This involves finding the best combination of design parameters to achieve desired performance characteristics.

- **Finance:** Optimizing investment portfolios, developing trading strategies, and managing financial risk. This involves finding the best combination of assets and investment strategies to maximize returns while minimizing risk.

- **Machine Learning:** Combining deep learning and genetic algorithms can lead to powerful solutions for complex problems, such as hyperparameter optimization and neural architecture search [19]. This involves using GAs to optimize the parameters and structure of deep learning models, potentially improving their performance and reducing the need for manual tuning.

- **Healthcare:** Optimizing treatment plans, developing drug discovery strategies, and analyzing medical images. This involves finding the best combination of treatments and medications to achieve desired health outcomes.

Challenges and Future Developments

- **Computational Cost:** Evaluating the fitness of each solution can be computationally expensive, especially for complex problems. This can limit their applicability in situations where computational resources are limited.

- **Parameter Tuning:** The performance of GAs can be sensitive to the choice of parameters, such as population size, crossover rate, and mutation rate. Finding the optimal parameter settings can require experimentation and expertise.

- **Premature Convergence:** If stuck in local optima, GAs can sometimes converge to suboptimal solutions. This can prevent them from finding the truly best solution to the problem.

Advantages and Disadvantages

Advantages	Disadvantages
1. Versatility: Can handle a wide range of optimization problems, including non-linear, multi-modal, and complex search spaces.	**1. Computationally Expensive:** Requires significant computational resources, especially for large populations or complex problems.
2. Global Search Capability: Explores the search space globally, reducing the risk of getting stuck in local optima.	**2. No Guarantee of Convergence:** Does not always find the optimal solution, and the quality of solutions may vary.
3. Adaptability: Easily adaptable to different types of problems by modifying the representation, operators, or fitness function.	**3. Sensitive to Parameter Tuning:** Performance heavily depends on parameters like population size, mutation rate, and crossover rate.
4. Parallelizable: Fitness evaluations can be performed in parallel, making it efficient for distributed computing environments.	**4. Slower Convergence:** May take many generations to converge to a good solution compared to deterministic algorithms.
5. Handles Discrete and Continuous Variables: Effective for both types of optimization problems, unlike some traditional methods.	**5. Requires Problem-Specific Design:** Needs careful design of the representation, fitness function, and genetic operators for each problem.
6. Robust to Noise: Performs well in noisy or dynamic	**6. Lack of Precision:** Produces approximate solutions rather than

Advantages	Disadvantages
environments where traditional methods struggle.	exact ones, which may not be acceptable in some applications.
7. Multi-Objective Optimization: Capable of optimizing multiple conflicting objectives simultaneously.	**7. Randomness Dependency:** Relies heavily on random processes, which may lead to inconsistent results across runs.
8. No Need for Gradient Information: Suitable for problems where the gradient is unavailable or difficult to compute.	**8. Overhead in Evaluation:** Fitness evaluation for complex problems can be computationally expensive and time-consuming.

Example Code:

```python
import numpy as np
import matplotlib.pyplot as plt
import random

# Define the fitness function
def fitness_function(x):
    """
    Example fitness function: maximize f(x) = x^2.
    """
    return x**2

# Initialize population
def initialize_population(size, bounds):
    """
    Initialize a population of individuals within the
given bounds.

    Parameters:
    size (int): Number of individuals in the population.
    bounds (tuple): The lower and upper bounds for the
individuals.
```

41

```
    Returns:
    numpy.ndarray: The initialized population.
    """

    return np.random.uniform(bounds[0], bounds[1], size)

# Selection
def select_parents(population, fitness):
    """
    Select two parents using a probability proportional
to fitness.

    Parameters:
    population (numpy.ndarray): The current population.
    fitness (numpy.ndarray): Fitness values of the
population.

    Returns:
    tuple: Two selected parents.
    """

    probabilities = fitness / fitness.sum()
    parents = np.random.choice(population, size=2,
p=probabilities)
    return parents

# Crossover
def crossover(parent1, parent2, crossover_rate=0.8):
    """
    Perform crossover between two parents to produce an
offspring.

    Parameters:
    parent1 (float): First parent.
    parent2 (float): Second parent.
    crossover_rate (float): Probability of crossover.

    Returns:
    float: The offspring.
    """

    if random.random() < crossover_rate:
        return (parent1 + parent2) / 2
```

```python
    return parent1 if random.random() < 0.5 else parent2

# Mutation
def mutate(individual, mutation_rate=0.1, bounds=(-10,
10)):
    """
    Apply mutation to an individual.

    Parameters:
    individual (float): The individual to mutate.
    mutation_rate (float): Probability of mutation.
    bounds (tuple): The lower and upper bounds for the
individual.

    Returns:
    float: The mutated individual.
    """
    if random.random() < mutation_rate:
        return np.random.uniform(bounds[0], bounds[1])
    return individual

# Genetic Algorithm
def genetic_algorithm(fitness_function, bounds,
population_size=20, generations=50):
    """
    Perform the Genetic Algorithm.

    Parameters:
    fitness_function (callable): The fitness function to
maximize.
    bounds (tuple): The lower and upper bounds for the
individuals.
    population_size (int): Number of individuals in the
population.
    generations (int): Number of generations to evolve.

    Returns:
    list: The history of the best fitness values over
generations.
    """
    # Initialize population
```

```python
    population = initialize_population(population_size,
bounds)
    fitness_history = []

    for generation in range(generations):
        # Evaluate fitness
        fitness = np.array([fitness_function(ind) for ind
in population])

        # Record the best fitness
        best_fitness = fitness.max()
        fitness_history.append(best_fitness)

        # Create a new population
        new_population = []
        for _ in range(population_size // 2):
            # Select parents
            parent1, parent2 = select_parents(population,
fitness)

            # Perform crossover
            offspring1 = crossover(parent1, parent2)
            offspring2 = crossover(parent2, parent1)

            # Apply mutation
            offspring1 = mutate(offspring1,
bounds=bounds)
            offspring2 = mutate(offspring2,
bounds=bounds)

            new_population.extend([offspring1,
offspring2])

        population = np.array(new_population)

    return fitness_history

# Plot the results
def plot_genetic_algorithm(fitness_history):
    """
    Plot the best fitness values over generations.
```

```
    Parameters:
    fitness_history (list): The best fitness values over
generations.
    """

    plt.figure(figsize=(10, 6))
    plt.plot(fitness_history, label="Best Fitness")
    plt.xlabel("Generation")
    plt.ylabel("Fitness")
    plt.title("Genetic Algorithm: Fitness Over
Generations")
    plt.legend()
    plt.grid()
    plt.show()

if __name__ == "__main__":
    # Parameters
    bounds = (-10, 10)   # Search space bounds
    population_size = 20
    generations = 50

    # Run Genetic Algorithm
    fitness_history = genetic_algorithm(fitness_function,
bounds, population_size, generations)

    # Plot results
    plot_genetic_algorithm(fitness_history)
```

Explanation:

1. **Fitness Function**:

    o The goal is to maximize $f(x)= x^2$

    o This function evaluates how "fit" an individual
       solution is.

2. **Population Initialization**:

- o A random population is generated within the specified bounds.

3. **Selection**:

   - o Parents are chosen using probabilities proportional to their fitness values.

4. **Crossover**:

   - o Averages the values of two parents to create offspring, with a certain crossover rate.

5. **Mutation**:

   - o Randomly alters offspring values with a small probability to maintain diversity in the population.

6. **Algorithm Iteration**:

   - o The population evolves over multiple generations, with fitness improving as stronger solutions are selected.

7. **Plot**:

   - o The plot visualizes how the best fitness improves over generations, showing the convergence of the algorithm.

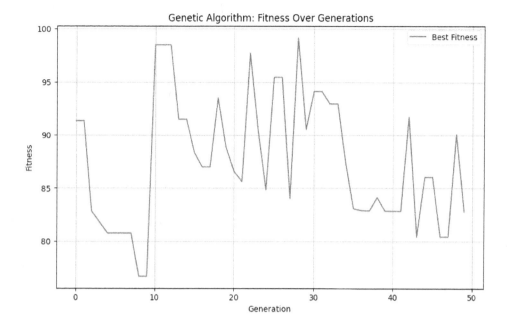

6. Fast Fourier Transform Algorithm

Definition	The Fast Fourier Transform (FFT) is an efficient algorithm to compute the Discrete Fourier Transform (DFT) and its inverse, enabling the transformation of a signal from the time domain to the frequency domain.
Main Domain	Signal Processing, Communications, Image Processing, and Scientific Computing.
Data Type	Numerical data, typically represented as discrete sequences of time-domain or spatial-domain signals.
Learning Paradigm	Deterministic algorithm; applies a divide-and-conquer strategy to reduce computational complexity.
Explainability	High explainability; the underlying mathematical principles (Fourier transforms) are well-understood, and the algorithm's steps are clear and interpretable.

The Fast Fourier Transform (FFT) is an algorithm that computes the Discrete Fourier Transform (DFT) of a sequence or its inverse (IDFT) [20]. The DFT decomposes a sequence of values into components of different frequencies, which is helpful in many fields, including signal processing, image analysis, and data compression. The FFT significantly reduces the computational complexity of computing the DFT, making it practical for real-world applications [21].

How the Fast Fourier Transform Works

The FFT achieves its speed by factorizing the DFT matrix into a product of sparse (mostly zero) factors [20]. This factorization reduces the computations required to compute the DFT from $O(n^2)$ to $O(n \log n)$, where n is the data size. This difference in speed can be enormous, especially for long data sets where n may be in the thousands or millions.

Impact and Applications

- **Signal Processing:** Analyzing and processing signals in audio, video, and communication systems. This involves decomposing signals into their frequency components to identify patterns, filter noise, and extract meaningful information.
- **Image Analysis:** Analyzing and processing images in medical imaging, computer vision, and pattern recognition. This involves transforming images into the frequency domain to enhance features, remove noise, and perform image compression.
- **Data Compression:** Compressing audio, video, and image files for efficient storage and transmission. This involves removing redundant information and representing the data more compactly.
- **Scientific Computing:** Solving differential equations, simulating

physical systems, and analyzing scientific data. This involves using the FFT to perform efficient calculations and analyze data in the frequency domain.

Challenges and Future Developments

- **Non-stationary Signals:** The FFT is most effective for stationary signals, where the statistical properties do not change over time. Analyzing non-stationary signals, where the frequency content changes over time, requires more sophisticated techniques.
- **Real-time Processing:** Performing FFT in real-time requires fast hardware and optimized algorithms, especially for high data rates or large FFT sizes. This can be challenging in applications where latency is critical.
- **Memory Requirements:** Storing and processing large datasets for FFT can require significant memory resources. This can be a limiting factor in applications with limited memory capacity.

Advantages and Disadvantages

Advantages	Disadvantages
1. **Efficiency:** Reduces the computational complexity of calculating the Discrete Fourier Transform (DFT) from $O(n^2)$ to $O(n \log n)$	1. **Requires Power-of-Two Length:** Many FFT implementations require the input size to be a power of two, which may necessitate padding and introduce inefficiencies.
2. **Widely Used:** Applicable in diverse fields such as signal	2. **Fixed Frequency Resolution:** The resolution is determined by the

Advantages	Disadvantages
processing, image processing, and scientific computing.	length of the input signal, limiting flexibility.
3. Accurate: Provides high precision for transforming signals between time and frequency domains.	**3. Assumes Periodicity:** Assumes the input signal is periodic, which can introduce artifacts (e.g., spectral leakage) for non-periodic signals.
4. Versatile: Can be applied to a variety of transformations, including 1D, 2D, and multidimensional Fourier transforms.	**4. Sensitivity to Noise:** FFT can amplify noise present in the signal, leading to less reliable results for noisy data.
5. Parallelizable: Well-suited for parallel computation, further speeding up large-scale transformations.	**5. Complex Number Output:** Produces complex numbers in the frequency domain, requiring additional steps for interpretation.
6. Real-Time Processing: Ideal for applications requiring real-time signal analysis, such as audio and communications systems.	**6. Memory Intensive:** Requires significant memory for large datasets, especially for multidimensional FFTs.
7. Easy to Implement: Standard libraries and tools make it straightforward to use in most programming languages.	**7. Boundary Effects:** Can introduce edge effects when analyzing finite-length signals without proper windowing.
8. Handles Large Data Efficiently: Capable of processing large datasets in manageable timeframes.	**8. Specialized Hardware May Be Needed:** Real-time applications often require dedicated hardware like DSPs (Digital Signal Processors).

Example Code:

```python
import numpy as np
import matplotlib.pyplot as plt

def generate_signal(frequencies, sampling_rate,
duration):
    """
    Generate a signal with given frequencies.

    Parameters:
    frequencies (list): List of frequencies to include in
    the signal.
    sampling_rate (int): Number of samples per second.
    duration (float): Duration of the signal in seconds.

    Returns:
    tuple: (time, signal) where time is the time array
    and signal is the combined signal.
    """
    time = np.linspace(0, duration, int(sampling_rate *
duration), endpoint=False)
    signal = np.sum([np.sin(2 * np.pi * freq * time) for
freq in frequencies], axis=0)
    return time, signal

def plot_signal(time, signal, title="Signal"):
    """
    Plot a time-domain signal.

    Parameters:
    time (numpy.ndarray): Time array.
    signal (numpy.ndarray): Signal array.
    title (str): Title of the plot.
    """
    plt.figure(figsize=(10, 4))
    plt.plot(time, signal, label="Signal")
    plt.title(title)
    plt.xlabel("Time [s]")
    plt.ylabel("Amplitude")
    plt.grid()
```

```python
    plt.legend()
    plt.show()

def plot_fft(signal, sampling_rate):
    """
    Plot the FFT of a signal.

    Parameters:
    signal (numpy.ndarray): Signal array.
    sampling_rate (int): Sampling rate of the signal.
    """
    # Perform FFT
    fft_result = np.fft.fft(signal)
    fft_freqs = np.fft.fftfreq(len(signal),
d=1/sampling_rate)

    # Only take the positive half of the spectrum
    positive_freqs = fft_freqs[:len(fft_result)//2]
    positive_magnitude =
np.abs(fft_result[:len(fft_result)//2])

    # Plot the FFT
    plt.figure(figsize=(10, 4))
    plt.plot(positive_freqs, positive_magnitude,
label="FFT Magnitude")
    plt.title("Fast Fourier Transform (FFT)")
    plt.xlabel("Frequency [Hz]")
    plt.ylabel("Magnitude")
    plt.grid()
    plt.legend()
    plt.show()

if __name__ == "__main__":
    # Parameters
    frequencies = [5, 50, 120]  # Frequencies in Hz
    sampling_rate = 1000  # Sampling rate in Hz
    duration = 2  # Duration in seconds

    # Generate the signal
    time, signal = generate_signal(frequencies,
sampling_rate, duration)
```

```
# Plot the time-domain signal
plot_signal(time, signal, title="Time-Domain Signal")

# Plot the frequency-domain signal using FFT
plot_fft(signal, sampling_rate)
```

Explanation:

1. **Signal Generation**:

   o A time-domain signal is created by summing sine waves of specified frequencies.

   o The **generate_signal** function uses **numpy** to create the time array and calculate the signal.

2. **Fast Fourier Transform (FFT)**:

   o The FFT is used to convert the time-domain signal into its frequency-domain representation.

   o **numpy.fft.fft** computes the FFT, and **numpy.fft.fftfreq** calculates the corresponding frequencies.

3. **Plotting**:

   o **Time-Domain Plot**: Shows the original signal over time.

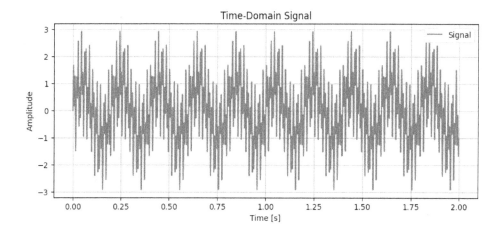

o **Frequency-Domain Plot**: Displays the magnitude of the FFT, which highlights the frequencies present in the signal.

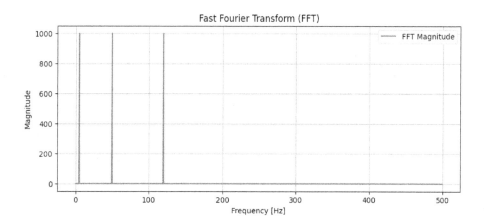

7. Support Vector Machine Algorithm

Definition	Support Vector Machine (SVM) is a supervised machine learning algorithm used for classification and regression tasks. It aims to find the hyperplane that best separates data points of different classes in a high-dimensional space.
Main Domain	Machine Learning, Pattern Recognition, and Data Mining.
Data Type	Numerical and categorical data; works on structured datasets and can handle both linearly and non-linearly separable data (via kernels).
Learning Paradigm	Supervised learning; constructs a hyperplane by maximizing the margin between data classes, with optional kernel tricks for non-linear boundaries.
Explainability	Medium explainability; while the basic concept of hyperplanes and margins is interpretable, the use of kernels and high-dimensional transformations can reduce interpretability.

A Support Vector Machine (SVM) is a supervised machine learning algorithm for classification and regression tasks [22]. It is particularly effective for high-dimensional data and can handle linear and non-linear classification problems. SVMs are widely used in various applications, including image classification, text classification, and bioinformatics.

How Support Vector Machines Work

SVMs aim to find the optimal hyperplane in an N-dimensional space that can effectively separate data points into different classes [22]. The hyperplane is the decision boundary that maximizes the margin between the closest points of other courses, known as support vectors.

SVMs can handle non-linearly separable data by using kernel functions to transform it into a higher-dimensional space where it becomes linearly separable [23]. This technique, known as the "kernel trick," allows SVMs to classify complex data effectively.

Impact and Applications

- **Image Classification:** Classifying images based on content, such as identifying objects, faces, or scenes. This is used in applications like image search, object detection, and facial recognition.
- **Text Classification:** Classifying text documents based on their topic, sentiment, or author. This is used in spam filtering, sentiment analysis, and document categorization applications.
- **Bioinformatics:** Analyzing biological data, such as gene expression data or protein sequences, to classify diseases or

predict drug responses. This helps researchers understand complex biological processes and develop new treatments.

- **Finance:** Detecting fraudulent transactions, predicting stock prices, and managing financial risk. This involves analyzing economic data to identify patterns and predict future trends.

Challenges and Future Developments

- **Scalability:** SVMs can be computationally expensive to train, especially for large datasets. This can limit their applicability in situations where computational resources are limited.
- **Parameter Tuning:** The performance of SVMs can be sensitive to the choice of parameters, such as the kernel type and regularization parameters. Finding the optimal parameter settings can require expertise and experimentation.
- **Interpretability:** Understanding the decision boundary of an SVM can be challenging, especially for non-linear kernels. This can make explaining the reasoning behind the SVM's predictions difficult.

Advantages and Disadvantages

Advantages	Disadvantages
1. Effective for High-Dimensional Data: Works well with datasets that have many features, even when the number of features exceeds the number of samples.	**1. Computationally Intensive:** Training can be slow for large datasets due to the quadratic optimization problem involved.

Advantages	Disadvantages
2. Robust to Overfitting: Effective in cases where there is a clear margin of separation between classes, especially in high-dimensional spaces.	**2. Sensitive to Kernel Choice:** The performance heavily depends on the choice of kernel and its parameters, requiring careful tuning.
3. Versatile: Can handle linear and non-linear classification tasks using different kernel functions (e.g., linear, polynomial, RBF).	**3. Not Suitable for Large Datasets:** Scales poorly with large datasets, as both memory and computation grow with the size of the dataset.
4. Effective for Binary Classification: Provides high accuracy and robustness for two-class classification problems.	**4. Limited in Multi-Class Problems:** While SVM can handle multi-class problems (e.g., one-vs-one, one-vs-rest), it is inherently designed for binary classification.
5. Margin Maximization: Ensures better generalization by finding the hyperplane with the maximum margin between classes.	**5. Requires Feature Scaling:** Input features need to be normalized or standardized for effective performance.
6. Handles Non-Linear Data: Using kernels, SVM can efficiently classify non-linear data.	**6. Hard to Interpret:** The model's decision boundary and feature importance are not as easily interpretable compared to other algorithms like decision trees.
7. Works Well for Small Datasets: Performs well on small datasets with a well-separated class structure.	**7. Sensitive to Outliers:** Outliers can significantly affect the position of the hyperplane and degrade performance.

Advantages	Disadvantages
8. Strong Theoretical Foundation: Based on statistical learning theory, ensuring a robust mathematical foundation.	**8. Memory Intensive:** Requires storing and processing all support vectors, which can become resource-intensive for large datasets.

Example Code:

```python
import numpy as np
import matplotlib.pyplot as plt
from sklearn.datasets import make_blobs
from sklearn.svm import SVC

def generate_data():
    """
    Generate a 2D dataset with two classes for
classification.

    Returns:
    tuple: (X, y) where X is the feature matrix and y is
the target vector.
    """
    X, y = make_blobs(n_samples=100, centers=2,
random_state=6, cluster_std=1.5)
    return X, y

def train_svm(X, y):
    """
    Train an SVM classifier on the provided data.

    Parameters:
    X (numpy.ndarray): Feature matrix.
    y (numpy.ndarray): Target vector.

    Returns:
    SVC: Trained SVM classifier.
    """
```

```python
    clf = SVC(kernel='linear', C=1.0)
    clf.fit(X, y)
    return clf

def plot_decision_boundary(clf, X, y):
    """
    Plot the decision boundary of the SVM classifier.

    Parameters:
    clf (SVC): Trained SVM classifier.
    X (numpy.ndarray): Feature matrix.
    y (numpy.ndarray): Target vector.
    """
    # Create a grid to evaluate the model
    x_min, x_max = X[:, 0].min() - 1, X[:, 0].max() + 1
    y_min, y_max = X[:, 1].min() - 1, X[:, 1].max() + 1
    xx, yy = np.meshgrid(np.arange(x_min, x_max, 0.01),
                         np.arange(y_min, y_max, 0.01))

    # Predict on the grid
    Z = clf.predict(np.c_[xx.ravel(), yy.ravel()])
    Z = Z.reshape(xx.shape)

    # Plot the decision boundary
    plt.figure(figsize=(10, 6))
    plt.contourf(xx, yy, Z, alpha=0.8,
cmap=plt.cm.coolwarm)

    # Plot the original data
    plt.scatter(X[:, 0], X[:, 1], c=y, edgecolor='k',
cmap=plt.cm.coolwarm)
    plt.title("SVM Decision Boundary")
    plt.xlabel("Feature 1")
    plt.ylabel("Feature 2")
    plt.grid()
    plt.show()

if __name__ == "__main__":
    # Generate synthetic data
    X, y = generate_data()
```

```
# Train SVM classifier
clf = train_svm(X, y)

# Plot decision boundary
plot_decision_boundary(clf, X, y)
```

Explanation:

1. **Data Generation**:

   o The **make_blobs** function creates a synthetic dataset with two distinct classes that can be classified using a linear boundary.

2. **Support Vector Machine (SVM)**:

   o The **SVC** class from **sklearn** is used with a linear kernel.

   o It identifies the hyperplane that best separates the classes with maximum margin.

3. **Decision Boundary Plot**:

   o A mesh grid is created to evaluate the SVM model across the feature space.

   o The decision boundary and the data points are plotted to visualize the classification.

4. **Example Output**:

- o The plot shows the two classes and the decision boundary separating them.

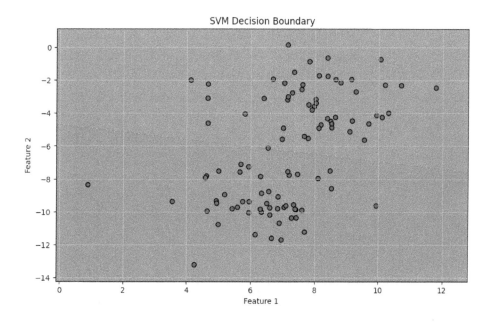

- o The margin (area between decision boundary and support vectors) highlights the SVM's functionality.

8. Backpropagation Algorithm

Definition	Backpropagation is a supervised learning algorithm used for training artificial neural networks by calculating the gradient of the loss function with respect to the weights through the chain rule of calculus.
Main Domain	Machine Learning, Deep Learning, and Neural Network Optimization.
Data Type	Numerical data; typically structured as feature vectors and corresponding labels for supervised tasks.
Learning Paradigm	Supervised learning; minimizes error by iteratively updating weights through gradient descent or its variants.
Explainability	Medium explainability; while the mathematical operations (e.g., gradient computation) are straightforward, the complex network architectures and large parameter spaces can make the overall model behavior hard to interpret.

Backpropagation is a key algorithm used to train artificial neural networks [24]. It is a supervised learning algorithm that adjusts the weights and biases of a neural network to minimize the difference between the network's predicted output and the actual output. Backpropagation is essential for optimizing deep learning models and has played a crucial role in advancing artificial intelligence.

How Backpropagation Works

Backpropagation propagates the error signal back through the network from the output layer to the input layer [25]. The error signal is calculated as the difference between predicted and actual output. The algorithm then adjusts the weights and biases of each neuron in the network to reduce the error signal.

This process is repeated for many iterations, with the network gradually learning to make more accurate predictions. Backpropagation often utilizes optimization algorithms like gradient descent or stochastic gradient descent to update the network's parameters efficiently.

Impact and Applications

- **Image Recognition:** Training neural networks to recognize objects, faces, and scenes in images. This is used in applications like image search, object detection, and self-driving cars.
- **Natural Language Processing:** Training neural networks to understand and generate human language, such as machine translation and summarization. This enables computers to communicate with humans more naturally.
- **Speech Recognition:** Training neural networks to recognize

spoken words and convert them into text. This is used in voice assistants, speech-to-text software, and voice search applications.

- **Robotics:** Training neural networks to control robots and enable them to perform complex tasks. This allows robots to learn from experience and adapt to new situations.

Challenges and Future Developments

- **Vanishing Gradients:** In deep networks, the gradients can become very small during backpropagation, making it difficult for the network to learn. This occurs because the error signal diminishes as it propagates through the layers.
- **Exploding Gradients:** The gradients can also become excessively large, causing the network to diverge during training. This occurs when the error signal amplifies and propagates back through the layers.
- **Overfitting:** If the network is too complex, it might memorize the training data instead of learning general patterns. This can lead to poor performance on new, unseen data.

Advantages and Disadvantages

Advantages	Disadvantages
1. Universal Applicability: Works for any differentiable activation function and is the backbone of training most neural networks.	**1. Computationally Intensive:** Training can be slow for large networks or datasets due to the iterative nature of the algorithm.
2. Efficient Gradient Computation: Uses the chain	**2. Sensitive to Hyperparameters:** Performance depends heavily on

Advantages	Disadvantages
rule to compute gradients efficiently, making it scalable for deep networks.	learning rate, batch size, and other hyperparameters, which require tuning.
3. Supports Deep Learning: Enables the training of multi-layer neural networks, which are essential for solving complex problems.	**3. Risk of Overfitting:** Can overfit the training data if the network is too complex or lacks proper regularization.
4. Widely Supported: Implemented in most machine learning frameworks (e.g., TensorFlow, PyTorch), making it accessible and easy to use.	**4. Vanishing Gradients:** Gradients can become very small in deep networks, leading to slow learning or failure to train effectively.
5. Adaptive Learning: Can learn features directly from raw data without requiring feature engineering.	**5. Exploding Gradients:** In some cases, gradients can become excessively large, destabilizing the training process.
6. Flexible Architecture: Can be applied to networks of varying sizes and architectures, including recurrent and convolutional networks.	**6. Black-Box Nature:** The internal workings of the network are not easily interpretable, making it difficult to understand the decision-making process.
7. Supports Transfer Learning: Pre-trained networks trained with backpropagation can be fine-tuned for new tasks.	**7. Requires Differentiable Functions:** All activation functions and layers must be differentiable, limiting the choice of architectures.
8. Proven Effectiveness: The foundation of modern deep learning, with applications in	**8. Memory Intensive:** Storing intermediate computations for backpropagation can be resource-

Advantages	Disadvantages
vision, NLP, and many other domains.	intensive for large models and datasets.

Example Code:

```python
import numpy as np
import matplotlib.pyplot as plt

# Define the activation function and its derivative
def sigmoid(x):
    return 1 / (1 + np.exp(-x))

def sigmoid_derivative(x):
    return x * (1 - x)

# Backpropagation Neural Network
def train_backpropagation(X, y, hidden_neurons=4,
epochs=10000, learning_rate=0.1):
    """
    Train a simple neural network using backpropagation.

    Parameters:
    X (numpy.ndarray): Input data.
    y (numpy.ndarray): Target data.
    hidden_neurons (int): Number of neurons in the hidden
layer.
    epochs (int): Number of training iterations.
    learning_rate (float): Learning rate for weight
updates.

    Returns:
    list: History of error for each epoch.
    """
    # Initialize weights and biases
    input_neurons = X.shape[1]
    output_neurons = y.shape[1]
```

```python
    weights_input_hidden = np.random.uniform(-1, 1,
(input_neurons, hidden_neurons))
    weights_hidden_output = np.random.uniform(-1, 1,
(hidden_neurons, output_neurons))
    bias_hidden = np.random.uniform(-1, 1, (1,
hidden_neurons))
    bias_output = np.random.uniform(-1, 1, (1,
output_neurons))

    error_history = []

    for epoch in range(epochs):
        # Forward pass
        hidden_input = np.dot(X, weights_input_hidden) +
bias_hidden
        hidden_output = sigmoid(hidden_input)
        final_input = np.dot(hidden_output,
weights_hidden_output) + bias_output
        final_output = sigmoid(final_input)

        # Calculate error
        error = y - final_output
        error_history.append(np.mean(np.abs(error)))

        # Backward pass
        d_output = error *
sigmoid_derivative(final_output)
        error_hidden_layer =
d_output.dot(weights_hidden_output.T)
        d_hidden_layer = error_hidden_layer *
sigmoid_derivative(hidden_output)

        # Update weights and biases
        weights_hidden_output +=
hidden_output.T.dot(d_output) * learning_rate
        weights_input_hidden += X.T.dot(d_hidden_layer) *
learning_rate
        bias_output += np.sum(d_output, axis=0,
keepdims=True) * learning_rate
        bias_hidden += np.sum(d_hidden_layer, axis=0,
keepdims=True) * learning_rate
```

```
    return error_history

# Plot the training error
def plot_training_error(error_history):
    """
    Plot the error history over epochs.

    Parameters:
    error_history (list): List of errors for each epoch.
    """
    plt.figure(figsize=(10, 6))
    plt.plot(error_history, label='Error')
    plt.xlabel("Epoch")
    plt.ylabel("Error")
    plt.title("Training Error Over Time")
    plt.legend()
    plt.grid()
    plt.show()

if __name__ == "__main__":
    # Example data (XOR problem)
    X = np.array([[0, 0], [0, 1], [1, 0], [1, 1]])
    y = np.array([[0], [1], [1], [0]])

    # Train the neural network
    error_history = train_backpropagation(X, y,
hidden_neurons=4, epochs=10000, learning_rate=0.1)

    # Plot the training error
    plot_training_error(error_history)
```

Explanation:

1. **Neural Network Structure**:

   o The network has an input layer, one hidden layer, and an output layer.

- o The number of neurons in the hidden layer is configurable.

2. **Activation Function**:

   - o The sigmoid function is used as the activation function for both hidden and output layers.

   - o Its derivative is used during the backward pass for weight updates.

3. **Forward Pass**:

   - o Input data is passed through the network to compute outputs.

4. **Backward Pass (Backpropagation)**:

   - o The error between the predicted output and the actual target is calculated.

   - o Gradients are computed and used to update weights and biases.

5. **Error History**:

   - o The mean absolute error is recorded for each epoch to monitor training progress.

6. **Plot:**

○ The training error is plotted to show how the error decreases over time, indicating the network is learning.

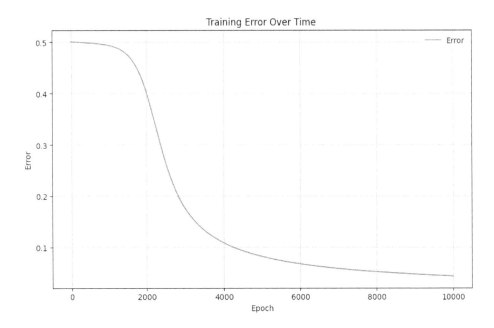

9. k-means Algorithm

Definition	k-means is an unsupervised clustering algorithm that partitions a dataset into k clusters by minimizing the sum of squared distances between data points and their corresponding cluster centroids.
Main Domain	Data Mining, Machine Learning, Pattern Recognition, and Image Segmentation.
Data Type	Numerical data; works on structured datasets, typically feature vectors in Euclidean space.
Learning Paradigm	Unsupervised learning; iteratively refines cluster assignments and centroid positions to minimize intra-cluster variance.
Explainability	High explainability; the algorithm's steps and outputs (clusters and centroids) are intuitive, though the choice of k and sensitivity to initialization can affect interpretability.

The k-means algorithm is an unsupervised machine learning algorithm for clustering data points into groups [26]. It partitions a dataset into k clusters, where each data point belongs to the cluster with the nearest mean. K-means is widely used in various applications, including market segmentation, image segmentation, and anomaly detection [27].

How the k-means Algorithm Works

The k-means algorithm starts by randomly selecting k initial centroids, the clusters' centers. It then assigns each data point to the cluster with the nearest centroid. After assigning all data points, the algorithm recalculates the centroids as the mean of the data points in each cluster.

This process of assigning data points and recalculating centroids is repeated until the centroids no longer change significantly or a predefined number of iterations has been reached. The final result is a set of k clusters, where each data point belongs to the cluster with the nearest centroid.

Impact and Applications

- **Market Segmentation:** Grouping customers into segments based on their purchasing behavior or demographics. This allows businesses to target specific customer groups with tailored marketing campaigns.
- **Image Segmentation:** Partitioning an image into regions based on color or texture. This is used in applications like image editing, object recognition, and medical imaging.
- **Anomaly Detection:** Identifying unusual data points that deviate significantly from the usual pattern. This is used in fraud detection, network security, and system monitoring applications.

- **Document Clustering:** Grouping documents based on their content or topic. This is used in information retrieval, document organization, and topic modeling applications.
- **Social Media:** Social media algorithms funnel specific content to particular audiences and encourage people to spend more time on platforms [28].

Challenges and Future Developments

- **Sensitivity to Initial Centroids:** The final clustering result can be sensitive to the initial choice of centroids. Different initializations can lead to different clustering outcomes.
- **Difficulty in Determining the Optimal Number of Clusters:** Choosing the optimal value for k can be challenging and may require experimentation or techniques like the elbow method or silhouette analysis.
- **Inability to Handle Non-spherical Clusters:** While k-means performs well with spherical or round-shaped clusters, it can struggle with clusters of varying sizes, densities, or non-spherical shapes [29].
- **Potential for Bias:** Like many algorithms, k-means can perpetuate existing biases if the data it is trained on reflects those biases. This can lead to unfair or discriminatory outcomes, particularly in social media applications where algorithms can contribute to the homogenization of culture and reinforce existing biases [30].

Advantages and Disadvantages

Advantages	Disadvantages
1. Simple and Easy to Implement: The algorithm is straightforward and easy to understand, making it accessible for a wide range of users.	**1. Sensitive to Initialization:** Poor initialization of centroids can lead to suboptimal clustering results.
2. Fast and Efficient: Has a time complexity of $O(n \cdot k \cdot i)$, where n is the number of data points, k is the number of clusters, and iii is the number of iterations.	**2. Assumes Spherical Clusters:** Assumes that clusters are spherical and equally sized, which may not always hold true for real-world data.
3. Scalable: Works well with large datasets when implemented efficiently.	**3. Sensitive to Outliers:** Outliers can distort the clustering results significantly by pulling centroids away from the actual cluster centers.
4. Works Well for Well-Separated Clusters: Effective for datasets with distinct and non-overlapping clusters.	**4. Fixed Number of Clusters:** Requires the number of clusters (k) to be specified beforehand, which can be challenging to determine.
5. Versatile Applications: Used in various domains such as image compression, market segmentation, and anomaly detection.	**5. Non-Deterministic Results:** The final output can vary due to the random initialization of centroids.
6. Handles High-Dimensional Data: Can be applied to data with many	**6. Cannot Handle Non-Linear Data:** Struggles with datasets

Advantages	Disadvantages
features, though performance may degrade in very high dimensions.	where clusters are non-linearly separable.
7. Easy to Interpret Results: Provides clear and intuitive cluster assignments.	**7. Requires Standardized Data:** Input features need to be scaled or normalized for meaningful results.
8. Widely Supported: Available in most data analysis and machine learning libraries, such as Scikit-learn.	**8. May Converge to Local Optima:** Without advanced initialization techniques (like k-means++), it might not find the global optimum.

Example Code:

```python
import numpy as np
import matplotlib.pyplot as plt
from sklearn.datasets import make_blobs
from sklearn.cluster import KMeans

def generate_data():
    """
    Generate a 2D dataset with three clusters for
clustering.

    Returns:
    tuple: (X, y) where X is the feature matrix and y is
the true labels.
    """
    X, y = make_blobs(n_samples=300, centers=3,
cluster_std=1.0, random_state=42)
    return X, y

def perform_kmeans(X, n_clusters):
    """
    Perform k-means clustering on the data.
```

```
    Parameters:
    X (numpy ndarray): Feature matrix.
    n_clusters (int): Number of clusters.

    Returns:
    tuple: (kmeans, y_pred) where kmeans is the KMeans
model and y_pred are the predicted labels.
    """
    kmeans = KMeans(n_clusters=n_clusters,
random_state=42)
    y_pred = kmeans.fit_predict(X)
    return kmeans, y_pred

def plot_clusters(X, y_pred, kmeans):
    """
    Plot the clusters and their centroids.

    Parameters:
    X (numpy.ndarray): Feature matrix.
    y_pred (numpy.ndarray): Predicted cluster labels.
    kmeans (KMeans): Trained KMeans model.
    """
    plt.figure(figsize=(10, 6))
    plt.scatter(X[:, 0], X[:, 1], c=y_pred,
cmap='viridis', s=50, alpha=0.6, label='Data Points')
    plt.scatter(kmeans.cluster_centers_[:, 0],
kmeans.cluster_centers_[:, 1],
                s=200, c='red', marker='X',
label='Centroids')
    plt.title("K-Means Clustering")
    plt.xlabel("Feature 1")
    plt.ylabel("Feature 2")
    plt.legend()
    plt.grid()
    plt.show()

if __name__ == "__main__":
    # Generate synthetic data
    X, y = generate_data()
```

```
# Perform k-means clustering
n_clusters = 3
kmeans, y_pred = perform_kmeans(X, n_clusters)

# Plot the resulting clusters
plot_clusters(X, y_pred, kmeans)
```

Explanation:

1. **Data Generation**:

   o Synthetic data is generated using make_blobs, which creates clusters of points in 2D space.

   o The number of samples, cluster centers, and spread of clusters are configurable.

2. **K-Means Clustering**:

   o The **KMeans** algorithm partitions the data into a specified number of clusters (**n_clusters**).

   o It iteratively assigns points to the nearest cluster center and updates the cluster centers to minimize the variance within clusters.

3. **Centroid Plot**:

   o Each data point is colored based on its cluster assignment.

   o Cluster centroids are marked with red *X* s.

9. k-means Algorithm

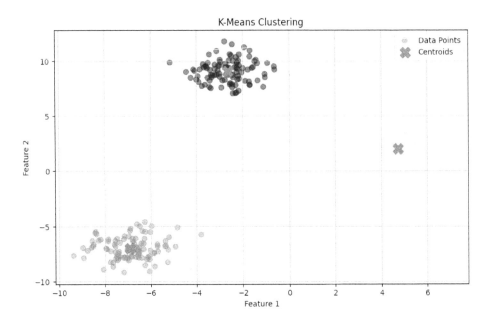

10. Apriori Algorithm

Definition	Apriori is an association rule mining algorithm that identifies frequent itemsets in transactional data and derives association rules based on the principle that any subset of a frequent itemset must also be frequent.
Main Domain	Data Mining, Market Basket Analysis, Recommender Systems, and Knowledge Discovery.
Data Type	Categorical data; transactional datasets (e.g., lists of items purchased together or event logs).
Learning Paradigm	Unsupervised learning; extracts patterns and relationships from data without labeled outputs.
Explainability	High explainability; the frequent itemsets and association rules are straightforward and easy to interpret, but large datasets can generate an overwhelming number of rules.

The Apriori algorithm is a data mining algorithm used to discover frequent item sets in dataset [31]. It is widely used in market basket analysis to identify items that are frequently purchased together.

It uses the "Apriori property" to reduce the search space and efficiently identify frequent item sets.

How the Apriori Algorithm Works

The Apriori algorithm starts by identifying all items that meet a minimum support threshold, the minimum frequency of occurrence in the dataset. It then generates candidate itemsets by combining frequent itemsets of size k to form itemsets of size k+1.

The algorithm prunes candidate itemsets that do not meet the minimum support threshold. This process continues until no more frequent item sets are generated. The final result is a set of frequent itemsets that can be used to generate association rules.

Impact and Applications

- **Market Basket Analysis:** Identifying items frequently purchased together, which can be used to improve product placement, recommend products to customers, and design targeted promotions. This helps businesses understand customer behavior and increase sales.
- **Healthcare:** Identifying patterns in medical data, such as symptoms or diagnoses that frequently occur together, can improve diagnosis and treatment. This can lead to more accurate diagnoses and more effective treatment plans.
- **Fraud Detection:** Identifying patterns in financial transactions that may indicate fraudulent activity. This helps businesses and financial institutions prevent fraud and protect their customers.
- **Recommendation Systems:** Recommending products or content to users based on their past behavior and preferences.

This improves user experience and helps businesses personalize their offerings.

Challenges and Future Developments

- **Computational Complexity:** The Apriori algorithm can be computationally expensive for large datasets with many items. This can limit its applicability in situations where computational resources are limited.
- **Memory Usage:** The algorithm can require significant memory to store candidate itemsets. This can be a problem for large datasets or limited memory resources.
- **Sensitivity to Support Threshold:** The choice of minimum support threshold can affect the number of frequent itemsets discovered. Setting the threshold too high may miss important patterns, while setting it too low may generate too many irrelevant itemsets.

Advantages and Disadvantages

Advantages	Disadvantages
1. Simple and Easy to Understand: The algorithm is conceptually straightforward and widely used for learning association rules.	**1. Computationally Expensive:** Performance degrades with large datasets due to the need to generate a large number of candidate itemsets.
2. Handles Categorical Data Well: Specifically designed for analyzing transactional data,	**2. Memory Intensive:** Requires storing and processing all candidate itemsets, leading to high memory usage.

Advantages	Disadvantages
making it ideal for market basket analysis.	
3. Flexible Support Thresholds: Allows users to define minimum support, enabling tailored analysis for specific use cases.	**3. Limited to Frequent Patterns:** Cannot find rare but important itemsets due to its dependence on minimum support.
4. Well-Supported: Implemented in various tools and libraries, making it accessible for practical applications.	**4. Generates Redundant Rules:** Often produces a large number of rules, many of which may be redundant or not actionable.
5. Effective for Small to Medium Datasets: Works efficiently for datasets of manageable size with moderate transaction counts.	**5. Poor Scalability:** Struggles with scalability for very large datasets or datasets with a high number of unique items.
6. Provides Interpretability: Results in clear, interpretable rules like if A, then B, aiding decision-making.	**6. Requires Discretized Data:** Continuous data must be preprocessed into discrete categories, which can lead to information loss.
7. Widely Applicable: Used in retail, healthcare, and other industries for association and pattern detection.	**7. Sensitive to Thresholds:** Results heavily depend on the minimum support and confidence thresholds, requiring careful tuning.
8. Proven Effectiveness: A foundational algorithm in data mining with a solid theoretical basis.	**8. Cannot Handle Dynamic Databases:** Needs to recompute rules entirely when the dataset changes.

Example Code:

```python
import pandas as pd
from mlxtend.preprocessing import TransactionEncoder
from mlxtend.frequent_patterns import apriori,
association_rules
import matplotlib.pyplot as plt

# Sample dataset (replace with your own)
dataset = [['Milk', 'Onion', 'Nutmeg', 'Kidney Beans',
'Eggs', 'Yogurt'],
            ['Dill', 'Onion', 'Nutmeg', 'Kidney Beans',
'Eggs', 'Yogurt'],
            ['Milk', 'Apple', 'Kidney Beans', 'Eggs'],
            ['Milk', 'Unicorn', 'Corn', 'Kidney Beans',
'Yogurt'],
            ['Corn', 'Onion', 'Onion', 'Kidney Beans',
'Ice cream', 'Eggs']]

# Preprocess the data
te = TransactionEncoder()
te_ary = te.fit(dataset).transform(dataset)
df = pd.DataFrame(te_ary, columns=te.columns_)

# Apply Apriori algorithm
frequent_itemsets = apriori(df, min_support=0.6,
use_colnames=True)

# Generate association rules
# Provide the num_itemsets argument
rules = association_rules(frequent_itemsets,
metric="lift", min_threshold=1,
num_itemsets=frequent_itemsets['itemsets'].apply(len))

# Print the rules
print(rules)

# Plot the rules (support vs confidence)
plt.scatter(rules['support'], rules['confidence'],
alpha=0.5)
plt.xlabel('Support')
```

```
plt.ylabel('Confidence')
plt.title('Association Rules')
plt.show()
```

Explanation:

1. Dataset Definition

- **Dataset**: A list of transactions, where each transaction is a list of items bought together.

3. Preprocessing the Data

- **TransactionEncoder**: Encodes the dataset into a one-hot-encoded matrix, where:

  o Rows represent transactions.

  o Columns represent items.

  o Values are 1 (item is present in the transaction) or 0 (item is absent).

- **Output Example**:

Apple	Corn	Dill	Eggs	Ice cream	KidneyBeans	Milk
Nutmeg	Onion	Unicorn	Yogurt			
0	0	0	0	1	0	1	1
1	1		0	1			
1	0	0	1	1	0		1	0
1	1		0	1...			

4. Applying the Apriori Algorithm

- **apriori**:

  - Identifies frequent itemsets (combinations of items that appear together in transactions) that satisfy the min_support threshold (≥ 60% in this case).

  - **use_colnames=True**: Ensures that the output displays item names instead of column indices.

- **Output Example**:

```
support                 itemsets
0   0.8             (Kidney Beans)
1   0.6                     (Eggs)
. . .
```

5. Generating Association Rules

- **association_rules**:

  - Generates rules such as: **If {A} is bought, {B} is also likely to be bought**.

  - **metric="lift"**: Uses lift (strength of the rule relative to random chance) as the metric.

  - **min_threshold=1**: Filters rules with a lift ≥ 1.

- **Output Example**:

```
antecedents   consequents   support   confidence   lift
0   (Milk)    (Kidney Beans)   0.8         1.0      1.25
```

6. Plotting Rules

- Creates a scatter plot of:

    - **Support** (x-axis): Proportion of transactions containing the itemset.

    - **Confidence** (y-axis): Likelihood of the consequent being bought given the antecedent.

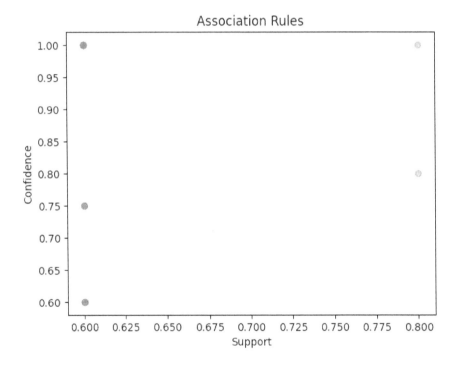

Expected Behavior

1. The code identifies frequent itemsets from the dataset.

2. It generates association rules that meet the lift threshold.

3. The scatter plot visualizes the relationship between support and confidence for these rules.

10. Apriori Algorithm

The Algorithmic Mirror: Reflections on Bias, Transparency, and Humanity

We stand at the precipice of a new era, where algorithms, intricate webs of logic and code, are increasingly shaping the contours of our world. These digital constructs hold immense promise, offering the potential to revolutionize fields from healthcare to finance, ushering in unprecedented advancements. Yet, as we entrust more of our lives to these invisible architects, we must pause and contemplate the profound ethical implications that arise from their pervasive influence. Algorithms, while seemingly neutral in their mathematical essence, are far from value-free; they are, in essence, a reflection of ourselves, mirroring our biases, our prejudices, and our aspirations.

One of the most pressing concerns is the potential for these powerful tools to exacerbate existing social inequalities. Like a distorting lens, algorithms trained on historical data can inadvertently amplify the inequities embedded within that data, perpetuating cycles of discrimination. In the hallowed halls of employment, algorithms meant to streamline hiring may unfairly disadvantage certain groups in their cold calculation, echoing the biases that have long haunted the workplace. Similarly, in the realm of finance, the very algorithms designed to assess risk may, in their reliance on past patterns, deny opportunities to individuals from marginalized communities, further entrenching economic disparities.

Beyond social justice, algorithms cast a long shadow over the fundamental right to privacy. These digital entities often thrive on a voracious diet of personal data, raising profound questions about surveillance, data security, and the potential for manipulation. We must ask ourselves: how can we ensure that in our pursuit of efficiency and progress, we do not sacrifice the sanctity of individual privacy at the altar of algorithmic optimization? How do we safeguard sensitive information from misuse, ensuring that the digital tapestry woven by algorithms does not ensnare us in a web of control?

We must be wary of the subtle yet insidious curating of our feeds, which can inadvertently construct echo chambers, feeding us only information confirming the ways in which algorithms can shape our perceptions and manipulate our choices. Social media, governed by algorithms that curate our feeds, can inadvertently construct echo chambers, feeding us only information that confirms our existing beliefs. While seemingly innocuous, this "filter bubble" effect can lead to intellectual isolation, societal polarization, and a profound erosion of informed nuanced discourse.

The Path Forward: Towards an Ethical Algorithmic Future

The challenges posed by this new era are as multifaceted as the algorithms themselves. We are called upon to navigate this uncharted territory with wisdom, foresight, and a deep commitment to ethical principles. Our task is to forge a path that allows us to harness the transformative power of algorithms while mitigating their potential harms. This necessitates:

- **Confronting Bias:** We must develop robust methodologies to identify and dismantle the biases embedded within algorithmic systems. This is not merely a technical challenge but a moral imperative – a commitment to ensuring these powerful tools are used to promote fairness, not perpetuate prejudice.

- **Safeguarding Privacy:** We must erect robust safeguards to protect individual privacy in an age of pervasive data collection. This requires a fundamental shift in our approach to data governance, one that prioritizes individual autonomy and agency over algorithms' insatiable appetite.

- **Cultivating Transparency:** Algorithms' decision-making processes must be rendered transparent and explainable. We must move beyond the "black box" paradigm, empowering individuals to understand how algorithmic decisions are made and fostering a sense of trust and accountability.

- **Establishing Accountability:** When algorithms err, causing harm or producing unjust outcomes, there must be precise mechanisms for accountability. This requires a framework for redress, ensuring that those affected by algorithmic missteps have recourse and that those responsible are accountable.

The journey ahead is complex, but our collective future depends on our ability to navigate it ethically. We must strive to create an algorithmic, technologically advanced but also just, equitable, and humane future. Let us strive to shape algorithms that reflect our ingenuity and our deepest values, ensuring that the algorithmic mirror reflects the best of humanity, not the worst.

We must not be passive recipients of algorithmic fate, but conscious architects of a digital future where technology serves justice, not the other way around.

Murat Durmus

Appendix: The Historical Backgrounds

PageRank Algorithm

The PageRank algorithm, the foundational technology behind Google's search engine dominance, has a surprisingly rich and somewhat contested history. While often attributed solely to Google's founders, Larry Page and Sergey Brin, its roots lie in earlier work on citation analysis and social network analysis.

Early Influences (Mid-20th Century):

- **Citation Analysis (1950s-1960s):**

    - **Eugene Garfield (Science Citation Index):** Garfield pioneered the field of bibliometrics with the Science Citation Index (SCI) in the 1960s. The SCI tracked citations between scientific papers, and the idea that highly cited papers are more important is a fundamental precursor to PageRank.

    - **Impact Factor:** Garfield's work led to the development of the "impact factor," a metric for assessing the importance of academic journals based on the frequency with which their articles are cited. This concept of using citations to measure influence is a clear predecessor to PageRank's link-based ranking.

- **Social Network Analysis (Sociometry):**

 ○ **Jacob Moreno (1930s):** Moreno's work on sociometry involved mapping social relationships and influence within groups. His techniques for analyzing social networks, though not directly linked to PageRank, share the concept of using relationships (links) to determine importance or authority.

○ **Katz Centrality (1953):** Developed by Leo Katz, this measure of a node's influence in a network considers not only direct connections but also indirect connections, weighted by a decay factor. This idea of influence propagating through a network is similar to how PageRank works.

Precursors to PageRank (1970s-1990s):

- **Hypertext Search Engines (Early 1990s):** Before Google, early search engines like Archie, Veronica, and Jughead primarily relied on keyword matching and directory structures. They lacked sophisticated methods for ranking the relevance of web pages.

- **The Hyper Search Engine (1996):** Massimo Marchiori developed the "Hyper Search" engine while at the University of Padua. His algorithm used the relationship between individual pages on a website to rank the website's overall importance. Marchiori later argued that

Google had incorporated ideas from his work, a claim that has been debated.

The Birth of PageRank at Stanford (1996-1998):

- **Larry Page and Sergey Brin:** While PhD students at Stanford University, Page and Brin conceived the idea of using the link structure of the World Wide Web to rank the importance of web pages. They recognized that a link from one page to another could be interpreted as a "vote" of confidence.

- **The BackRub Project (1996):** Page initially worked on a project called BackRub, which explored the "backlinks" pointing to a given web page. This project evolved into the PageRank algorithm.

- **"The Anatomy of a Large-Scale Hypertextual Web Search Engine" (1998):** In this seminal paper, Page and Brin outlined the PageRank algorithm and presented it as a key component of their new search engine, which they later named Google. They described PageRank as a method for computing a ranking of every web page based on the "web of trust" created by hyperlinks. The formula considers both the number and the quality of incoming links to determine a page's PageRank score.

- **Patent (1998):** Stanford University filed for a patent on the PageRank algorithm, listing Lawrence Page as the inventor. This patent has been a subject of some controversy, as some argue that it doesn't fully acknowledge the contributions of earlier work.

Post-PageRank and Google's Evolution:

- **Beyond PageRank:** While PageRank was a critical innovation, Google's search algorithms have become vastly more complex over time. They now incorporate hundreds of factors, including content relevance, user behavior, machine learning, and many other signals to determine search rankings.

- **RankBrain (2015):** This AI-based system is one of the major updates that interprets the meaning behind search queries and matches them to relevant results, even if the query doesn't contain the exact keywords found on the page.

- **Continued Evolution:** Google continually updates its algorithms to combat spam, improve relevance, and adapt to the evolving nature of the web.

RSA Algorithm

The RSA algorithm, a cornerstone of modern cryptography and internet security, has a history intertwined with the worlds of academia, government secrecy, and the burgeoning field of public-key cryptography.

Early Developments in Cryptography (Pre-1970s):

- **Symmetric-Key Cryptography:** Historically, cryptography relied on symmetric-key algorithms. In these systems, the same secret key is used for both encryption and decryption. The challenge lies in securely distributing the key between parties.

- **The Key Distribution Problem:** As communication networks grew, the problem of securely distributing keys became a major bottleneck for symmetric-key cryptography. How could two parties who had never met establish a shared secret without a secure channel?

The Dawn of Public-Key Cryptography (Mid-1970s):

- **Whitfield Diffie and Martin Hellman (1976):** In their groundbreaking paper "New Directions in Cryptography," Diffie and Hellman introduced the revolutionary concept of public-key cryptography. They proposed a system where each user would have a pair of keys: a public key for encryption and a private key for decryption.

- **The Diffie-Hellman Key Exchange:** They also presented a method for two parties to securely exchange a secret key over an insecure channel, solving the key distribution problem. However, their method was limited to key exchange and didn't provide a way to encrypt and decrypt messages.

- **The Search for a Trapdoor Function:** Diffie and Hellman outlined the need for a "trapdoor one-way function" – a mathematical function that is easy to compute in one direction but difficult to reverse without special information (the "trapdoor"). This function would be the basis for a true public-key encryption scheme.

The Invention of RSA (1977):

- **Rivest, Shamir, and Adleman at MIT:** Inspired by Diffie and Hellman's work, Ron Rivest, Adi Shamir, and Leonard Adleman at MIT embarked on a quest to find a practical trapdoor function.

- **The Breakthrough:** After many attempts, they discovered a solution based on the difficulty of factoring large numbers. Their algorithm, named RSA after their initials, was published in 1977 in "A Method for Obtaining Digital Signatures and Public-Key Cryptosystems".

- **How RSA Works:**

  o **Key Generation:** RSA relies on the fact that it's easy to multiply two large prime numbers but extremely difficult to factor the product back into the original primes. Each user generates a public key consisting of the product of two large primes and a related exponent, and a private key consisting of the original prime numbers and a different exponent.

- ○ **Encryption:** To encrypt a message, the sender uses the recipient's public key.

- ○ **Decryption:** Only the recipient, with the knowledge of the private key (the original prime factors), can efficiently decrypt the message.

- **Impact:** RSA provided the first practical implementation of public-key cryptography for both encryption and digital signatures. It revolutionized secure communication and became a foundation for internet security.

Secret History at GCHQ (Early 1970s - Revealed 1997):

- **James H. Ellis:** In the early 1970s, James H. Ellis, a British cryptographer working at the Government Communications Headquarters (GCHQ), conceived of the possibility of "non-secret encryption" (public-key cryptography) as early as 1969. He wrote an internal paper titled "The Possibility of Secure Non-Secret Digital Encryption" in 1970, but it was classified and not released publicly.

- **Clifford Cocks:** Building on Ellis's ideas, another GCHQ mathematician, Clifford Cocks, developed a specific encryption scheme in 1973 that was essentially equivalent to RSA. Cocks' work was also classified, written internally as "A Note on Non-Secret Encryption."

- **Malcolm Williamson:** A third GCHQ mathematician, Malcolm Williamson developed a key-exchange protocol similar to the Diffie-Hellman key exchange in 1974.

- **Declassification:** The GCHQ work remained classified until 1997 when the British government finally declassified the relevant documents. This revealed that the fundamental concepts of public-key cryptography, and even an algorithm similar to RSA, had been discovered within the intelligence community several years before the independent invention at MIT.

RSA's Legacy and Continued Importance:

- **Commercialization and RSA Security:** Rivest, Shamir, and Adleman founded RSA Security in 1982 to commercialize their algorithm. RSA became widely adopted for securing online transactions, email, and other sensitive data.

- **Patenting and Licensing:** RSA Security held a patent on the RSA algorithm in the United States until 2000, which generated significant licensing revenue and also created some controversy within the cryptographic community.

- **Modern Cryptography:** While RSA remains widely used, newer cryptographic algorithms like Elliptic Curve Cryptography (ECC) have gained popularity due to their efficiency, especially for smaller key sizes.

- **Quantum Computing Threat:** The potential development of large-scale quantum computers poses a significant threat to RSA, as Shor's algorithm (a quantum algorithm) can efficiently factor large numbers, breaking the security of RSA. This has led to research and development of post-quantum cryptography, which aims to develop algorithms resistant to attacks from quantum computers.

Linear programming

Linear programming (LP) has a rich history marked by contributions from mathematicians, economists, and computer scientists. Its development was driven by both theoretical considerations and the practical need to solve complex resource allocation problems, particularly during and after World War II.

Here's a breakdown of the historical background of linear programming:

Early Precursors (18th and 19th Centuries):

- He developed a method, later known as Fourier-Motzkin elimination, for solving systems of linear inequalities, which can be seen as a rudimentary form of LP.

- **Farkas (Late 19th/Early 20th Century):** The Hungarian mathematician Julius Farkas developed fundamental theorems on linear inequalities, now known as Farkas' lemma, which are crucial for understanding duality in linear programming.

Early 20th Century Developments:

- **Kantorovich (1930s):** The Soviet mathematician and economist Leonid Kantorovich is considered one of the key pioneers of linear programming. In 1939, he formulated and solved a problem related to the optimal allocation of resources in plywood production using linear programming techniques. He recognized the broad applicability of this approach to various economic planning problems. However, his work was largely unknown outside the Soviet Union for many years.

- **Koopmans (1940s):** The Dutch-American economist Tjalling Koopmans independently worked on similar problems related to optimal transportation and resource allocation during World War II. He later collaborated with Kantorovich, and they shared the 1975 Nobel Prize in Economics for their contributions to the theory of optimal allocation of resources.

- **Leontief (1930s-1940s):** Wassily Leontief, another Nobel laureate in Economics, developed input-output models to analyze the interdependencies between different sectors of an economy. While not directly linear programming, his work provided a framework for formulating economic problems that could be solved using LP techniques.

The Development of the Simplex Method (1947):

- **George Dantzig:** The American mathematician George Dantzig is widely regarded as the "father of linear programming." While working for the U.S. Air Force during World War II, he was tasked with developing methods for planning and scheduling complex military operations. In

1947, he formulated the general linear programming problem and developed the **simplex method**, an efficient algorithm for solving it.

- **The Simplex Method's Impact:** The simplex method was a breakthrough. It provided a systematic way to find optimal solutions to linear programming problems by iteratively moving from one vertex of the feasible region (defined by the constraints) to a neighboring vertex with a better objective function value until the optimum is reached.

- **Early Applications:** The simplex method was initially applied to military logistics and planning problems, but its potential for solving a wide range of optimization problems in various industries quickly became apparent.

Post-War Developments and Refinements (1950s-Present):

- **Duality Theory:** John von Neumann, a renowned mathematician, made significant contributions to the theory of duality in linear programming. Duality theory provides important insights into the structure of LP problems and has practical implications for sensitivity analysis and algorithm development.

- **Computational Advances:** The development of digital computers in the 1950s and beyond played a crucial role in making linear programming a practical tool for solving large-scale real-world problems.

- **Interior-Point Methods (1980s):** In 1984, Narendra Karmarkar introduced a new class of algorithms called interior-point methods for solving linear programming problems. These methods, unlike the simplex method, approach the optimal solution from the interior of the feasible region. Interior-point methods proved to be more efficient than the simplex method for certain types of large-scale problems.

- **Software and Applications:** Numerous software packages have been developed to implement the simplex method, interior-point methods, and other LP algorithms. Linear programming is now widely used in diverse fields such as operations research, economics, finance, engineering, transportation, manufacturing, and many others.

- **Continued Research:** Research on linear programming continues to this day, focusing on developing more efficient algorithms, handling larger and more complex problems, and exploring connections to other areas of optimization and mathematics.

MONTE CARLO ALGORITHM

The Monte Carlo method has a history rooted in statistical physics, the Manhattan Project, and the advent of the modern computer.

Early Roots (Pre-20th Century):

- **Buffon's Needle Problem (1777):** This is often cited as one of the earliest examples of a problem solved using a probabilistic method that foreshadowed Monte Carlo. Georges-Louis Leclerc, Comte de Buffon, posed the question: If a needle of length l is dropped randomly onto a floor with parallel lines spaced d units apart (where $d > l$), what is the probability that the needle will cross a line? The solution involves geometric probability and can be used to estimate the value of π.

- **Lord Kelvin and Statistical Sampling:** Lord Kelvin, in the late 19th century, used methods that could be considered precursors to Monte Carlo simulations in his work on the kinetic theory of gases. He occasionally used random sampling to analyze the behavior of molecules.

- **Enrico Fermi (1930s):** Before the widespread use of the term "Monte Carlo," Enrico Fermi, the renowned physicist, used random sampling techniques to study neutron diffusion. However, he did not formalize or publish these methods.

The Birth of the Monte Carlo Method (1940s):

- **The Manhattan Project:** The development of the atomic bomb during World War II at Los Alamos National Laboratory provided the crucial impetus for the formalization of the Monte Carlo method. Scientists like Stanislaw Ulam, John von Neumann, and Nicholas Metropolis faced complex problems in neutron diffusion and nuclear fission that were difficult or impossible to solve using deterministic methods.

- **Stanislaw Ulam's Solitaire Realization:** Ulam is often credited with the key insight that led to the Monte Carlo method. While playing solitaire during a period of illness, he wondered about the probability of successfully completing a game. He realized that instead of trying to calculate all possible combinations of card moves, it would be easier to simply play the game many times, recording the outcomes to estimate the probability. This idea of using random sampling to approximate a solution became the cornerstone of the Monte Carlo method.

- **John von Neumann's Contribution:** Von Neumann, a brilliant mathematician and one of the pioneers of computer science, recognized the potential of Ulam's idea and collaborated with him to develop it further. He saw the connection to the neutron diffusion problems they were facing in the Manhattan Project. Von Neumann was instrumental in formalizing the method and programming it on the ENIAC (Electronic Numerical Integrator and Computer), one of the first electronic general-purpose computers.

- **Nicholas Metropolis and the Name "Monte Carlo":** Metropolis, another key figure at Los Alamos, suggested the name "Monte Carlo" for the method, a reference to the famous Monte Carlo Casino in Monaco, known for its games of chance. The name was fitting given the method's reliance on randomness. He was also involved in developing the ENIAC programs.

- **The Metropolis Algorithm (1953):** Metropolis, along with Arianna W. Rosenbluth, Marshall Rosenbluth, Augusta H. Teller, and Edward Teller (the "father of the hydrogen bomb"), published the paper "Equation of State Calculations by Fast Computing Machines," which introduced the Metropolis algorithm (now known as Metropolis-Hastings), a specific and widely used Markov Chain Monte Carlo (MCMC) method.

Post-War Developments and Expansion (1950s-Present):

- **Increased Use with Computers:** The increasing availability and power of computers in the decades following World War II made Monte Carlo methods much more practical and led to their rapid adoption in various fields.

- **Applications Beyond Physics:** While initially developed for problems in physics, Monte Carlo methods found applications in numerous other areas, including operations research, finance, engineering, biology, computer graphics, and many more.

- **Markov Chain Monte Carlo (MCMC):** The development of MCMC methods, particularly the Metropolis-Hastings algorithm and the Gibbs sampler, revolutionized Bayesian statistics and other fields by enabling the sampling from complex, high-dimensional probability distributions.

- **Quasi-Monte Carlo:** Research into quasi-Monte Carlo methods, which use deterministic sequences instead of random numbers to improve convergence rates, has further enhanced the efficiency of Monte Carlo simulations in certain applications.

Genetic Algorithm

The Genetic Algorithm (GA) has a history rooted in the early days of computer science, artificial intelligence, and evolutionary biology.

Early Influences (1950s and 1960s):

- **Early Evolutionary Computation:** The idea of using principles of evolution to solve computational problems emerged in the 1950s and early 1960s. Several researchers explored different approaches to simulating evolution on computers:

    o **Nils Aall Barricelli (1954):** Conducted early experiments on symbiogenesis and evolution using computers at the Institute for Advanced Study in Princeton.

    o **Alex Fraser (1957):** Published a series of papers on simulating artificial selection of organisms with multiple loci controlling a measurable trait.

    o **Hans-Joachim Bremermann (1962):** Focused on optimization through evolution and recombination, introducing ideas like population-based search and the use of genetic operators.

    o **Richard Friedberg (1958):** Attempted to evolve computer programs through a process of mutation and selection, but with limited success.

113

- **The Rise of Artificial Intelligence:** The 1960s saw a surge of interest in artificial intelligence, and researchers were exploring various approaches to creating intelligent machines. Evolutionary computation was one of the avenues being investigated.

John Holland and the Formalization of Genetic Algorithms (1960s-1975):

- **John Holland's Vision:** John Holland, a professor at the University of Michigan, is considered the father of genetic algorithms. He was interested in understanding the adaptive processes of natural systems and how they could be applied to artificial systems. He was particularly fascinated by the robustness and adaptability of biological evolution.

- **"Adaptation in Natural and Artificial Systems" (1975):** Holland's seminal book, published in 1975, formally introduced genetic algorithms to the world. He presented a theoretical framework for GAs, drawing analogies between biological evolution and computational problem-solving. He introduced key concepts such as:

  - **Chromosomes and Genes:** Representing solutions as strings of bits (chromosomes) analogous to biological chromosomes, with individual bits representing genes.

- **Fitness Function:** Evaluating the quality of a solution using a fitness function, similar to how natural selection favors organisms with higher fitness.

- **Genetic Operators:** Using operators like selection, crossover (recombination), and mutation to create new generations of solutions, mimicking the processes of natural selection and genetic variation.

- **Schema Theorem:** Holland also developed the Schema Theorem, a theoretical result that helps explain how GAs explore the search space and converge towards optimal solutions.

- **The First PhD on GAs (1967):** Kenneth De Jong, a student of Holland, implemented and tested the Genetic Algorithm for his PhD thesis. He showed how GAs can be applied for function optimization.

Early Applications and Development (1970s-1980s):

- **De Jong's Function Optimization:** Kenneth De Jong's dissertation demonstrated the effectiveness of GAs on a set of test functions, establishing their potential for optimization problems.

- **The Traveling Salesman Problem:** John Grefenstette, another of Holland's students, applied GAs to the classic Traveling Salesman Problem, a well-known combinatorial optimization problem.

- **Growing Interest:** In the 1980s, interest in GAs grew rapidly, with researchers exploring various applications and developing new techniques to improve their performance.

- **The International Conference on Genetic Algorithms (ICGA):** The first ICGA was held in 1985, providing a forum for researchers to share their work and advance the field.

Further Developments and Expansion (1990s-Present):

- **Genetic Programming:** John Koza, building on Holland's work, developed genetic programming, which uses similar principles to evolve computer programs rather than fixed-length strings.

- **Evolution Strategies and Evolutionary Programming:** Other branches of evolutionary computation, such as evolution strategies (developed in Germany by Ingo Rechenberg and Hans-Paul Schwefel) and evolutionary programming (developed in the US by Lawrence J. Fogel), also gained prominence, offering alternative approaches to simulating evolution.

- **Hybrid Algorithms:** Researchers began to develop hybrid algorithms that combined GAs with other optimization techniques, such as simulated annealing and local search, to achieve better performance.

- **Multi-Objective Optimization:** GAs were extended to handle multi-objective optimization problems, where multiple conflicting objectives need to be optimized simultaneously.

- **Real-World Applications:** GAs have been successfully applied to a wide range of real-world problems in various domains, including engineering design, finance, scheduling, robotics, bioinformatics, and many others.

- **Continued Research:** Research on GAs continues today, focusing on areas such as improving their efficiency, developing new genetic operators, understanding their theoretical foundations, and exploring new applications.

The Fast Fourier Transform (FFT) Algorithm

The Fast Fourier Transform (FFT) algorithm is a cornerstone of modern computing, impacting fields ranging from signal processing and data analysis to solving partial differential equations and even multiplying large numbers. Its history is a fascinating journey spanning centuries, highlighting key contributions from mathematicians and engineers across different eras.

Early Roots (Pre-1805):

- **Rudimentary Analysis:** While not an FFT in the modern sense, early forms of harmonic analysis can be traced back to ancient Babylonian astronomers who analyzed periodicities in celestial phenomena.

- **Interpolation Techniques:** Mathematicians in the 17th and 18th centuries, like Newton and Lagrange, developed interpolation techniques which are related to Fourier analysis. These methods involved representing functions using a finite set of sampled points.

Gauss's Contribution (1805):

- **Unpublished Manuscript:** The earliest known explicit description of an FFT algorithm was found in the unpublished work of Carl Friedrich Gauss in 1805. He developed it to interpolate the orbits of asteroids from sample observations. His method was quite similar to the later Cooley-Tukey algorithm but was not published during his lifetime and was only rediscovered after the widespread adoption of the FFT in the 1960s. This work also predated Fourier's publication on harmonic analysis in 1807.

19th and Early 20th Century Developments:

- **Fourier's Work (1807-1822):** Joseph Fourier's groundbreaking work on the analytical theory of heat introduced the concept of representing functions as a sum of trigonometric functions (Fourier series). This laid the mathematical foundation for the later development of the FFT.

- **Limited Practical Use:** While the theoretical groundwork was in place, the practical application of Fourier analysis remained limited due to the substantial computational effort required for calculating the Fourier coefficients. The discrete Fourier transform (DFT), though conceptually known, was computationally very expensive for large datasets.

- **Runge and König (1924):** Carl Runge, along with his student, contributed improvements to the efficiency of calculating Fourier series, foreshadowing the FFT.

The Cooley-Tukey Algorithm (1965):

- **Rediscovery and Impact:** The development that revolutionized the field was the 1965 publication of the Cooley-Tukey algorithm by James Cooley and John Tukey. They rediscovered and popularized a method for calculating the DFT with significantly improved efficiency. Their algorithm reduced the computational complexity from O(N^2) for a direct DFT to O(N log N), making it feasible to analyze much larger datasets.

- **The Cold War Context:** Tukey reportedly developed the idea while working on problems related to detecting nuclear tests from seismic data as part of the US effort during the Cold War.

- **Rapid Adoption:** The Cooley-Tukey FFT algorithm was rapidly adopted in numerous fields due to the burgeoning use of digital computers. It became the workhorse of digital signal processing, image analysis, and many other areas.

Further Developments and Refinements:

- **Other FFT Algorithms:** Since 1965, numerous other FFT algorithms have been developed, including the Radix-4 FFT, Split-Radix FFT, Winograd FFT, and others. These algorithms offer further improvements in specific situations, often for particular data sizes or hardware architectures.

- **Hardware Implementations:** FFTs are often implemented directly in hardware (e.g., in digital signal processors and FPGAs) for performance-critical applications.

The Support Vector Machine (SVM) Algorithm

The Support Vector Machine (SVM) algorithm, a powerful and versatile tool in machine learning used for classification, regression, and outlier detection, has a history rooted in statistical learning theory and optimization. Here's a breakdown of its key milestones:

Early Foundations (1960s):

- **Vapnik and Chervonenkis's Work (Early 1960s):** The theoretical foundations of SVMs were laid in the early 1960s by Vladimir Vapnik and Alexey Chervonenkis in the Soviet Union. They were developing the field of statistical learning theory, focusing on the problem of pattern recognition. Their work introduced key concepts such as:

    o **Empirical Risk Minimization:** The idea of finding a model that minimizes the error on the training data.

    o **Structural Risk Minimization:** A principle that balances the model's complexity with its performance on the training data to prevent overfitting (where the model performs well on training data but poorly on unseen data).

    o **Vapnik-Chervonenkis (VC) Dimension:** A measure of the capacity or complexity of a learning machine. This concept is crucial for understanding generalization ability (how well a model will perform on new, unseen data).

- **The Linear Separator (1963):** In his early work, Vladimir Vapnik proposes an algorithm that finds the optimal separating hyperplane between two classes of data, in the case where the classes are linearly separable. This work introduces the concept of the margin (the distance between the hyperplane and the nearest data points) and the idea of maximizing this margin for better generalization.

Development of the SVM (1992-1995):

- **Boser, Guyon, and Vapnik (1992):** Bernhard Boser, Isabelle Guyon, and Vladimir Vapnik, working at AT&T Bell Laboratories, extended the earlier work on optimal separating hyperplanes to handle non-linearly separable data. They introduced the "kernel trick" in their 1992 paper, "A Training Algorithm for Optimal Margin Classifiers."

  - **The Kernel Trick:** This crucial innovation allows SVMs to efficiently find non-linear decision boundaries by implicitly mapping the data into a higher-dimensional feature space where the data might be linearly separable. The kernel function computes the similarity between data points in the original space without explicitly performing the mapping, thus avoiding the computational cost of working in the high-dimensional space.

- **Corinna Cortes and Vapnik (1995):** Corinna Cortes and Vladimir Vapnik further developed the SVM algorithm by introducing the "soft margin" concept in their 1995 paper, "Support-Vector Networks."

    o **Soft Margin:** This extension allows for some misclassification errors in the training data, making the SVM more robust to noise and outliers. It introduces a penalty parameter that controls the trade-off between maximizing the margin and minimizing the classification errors.

    o **Support Vectors:** This is also where the algorithm gets its name. The data points closest to the decision boundary which influence it the most are called "support vectors"

Popularization and Applications (Late 1990s - Present):

- **Performance and Efficiency:** SVMs quickly gained popularity in the machine learning community due to their strong theoretical foundations, excellent generalization performance, and ability to handle high-dimensional data. They often outperformed existing methods like neural networks on various benchmark datasets.

- **LIBSVM and Other Software:** The development of efficient software implementations, such as LIBSVM (developed by Chih-Chung Chang and Chih-Jen Lin), made SVMs more accessible to practitioners.

- **Wide Range of Applications:** SVMs have been successfully applied to a wide range of real-world problems, including:

    o **Image Recognition and Computer Vision:** Object detection, face recognition, image classification.

    o **Text and Hypertext Categorization:** Spam filtering, sentiment analysis, document classification.

    o **Bioinformatics:** Protein classification, gene expression analysis, cancer diagnosis.

    o **Finance:** Credit scoring, fraud detection, stock market prediction.

    o **Other Areas:** Handwriting recognition, medical diagnosis, remote sensing, and many more.

Ongoing Research and Developments:

- **Kernel Selection and Design:** Research continues on developing new and more effective kernel functions tailored to specific types of data and problems.

- **Scaling to Large Datasets:** Efforts are being made to improve the scalability of SVMs to handle very large datasets, including online learning algorithms and distributed implementations.

- **Connections to Deep Learning:** While SVMs and deep learning are often seen as distinct approaches, there is growing interest in exploring connections and hybrid models that combine the strengths of both.

- **Theoretical Advances:** Researchers continue to refine the theoretical understanding of SVMs, exploring topics such as generalization bounds, regularization, and the relationship to other learning algorithms.

The Backpropagation Algorithm

The backpropagation algorithm, the cornerstone of training artificial neural networks, has a history that's more nuanced and distributed than often portrayed. It wasn't a single "Eureka!" moment but rather a gradual development built upon the contributions of several researchers across different decades.

Here's a breakdown of the key milestones in the history of backpropagation:

Early Foundations (1960s - Early 1970s):

- **The Chain Rule:** The mathematical foundation of backpropagation is the chain rule of calculus, which dates back to Leibniz and Newton in the 17th century. The chain rule allows us to calculate the derivative of a composite function.

- **Early Optimizers: (1960s):** Early optimization methods, such as those developed by Kelley and Bryson et al. using optimal control theory, were precursors to backpropagation. They were based on the calculus of variations and dynamic programming, and could calculate gradients to update parameters in simple systems, but these did not gain traction in the neural network community.

- **Stephen Werbos's Work (1974):** In his 1974 PhD thesis at Harvard, Paul Werbos proposed a method that could be used to efficiently calculate gradients in a multi-layered system, which is essentially backpropagation. However, his work was largely overlooked at the time, as the field of neural networks was experiencing a period of reduced interest (the "AI winter"). Werbos himself moved to other fields, as his work didn't attract attention until much later.

The Development of Backpropagation (Mid-1980s):

- **Rumelhart, Hinton, and Williams (1986):** The most widely recognized development of backpropagation came in 1986 with the publication of the seminal paper "Learning representations by back-propagating errors" by David Rumelhart, Geoffrey Hinton, and Ronald Williams. They independently rediscovered and popularized the algorithm, demonstrating its effectiveness in training multi-layer perceptrons (MLPs), a type of feedforward neural network. They clearly showed how to calculate the error gradient and use it to update the network's weights. They also made clear the conditions under which the algorithm was applicable, most notably that all the activation functions be differentiable.

- **The PDP Group:** This work was part of a larger research effort by the Parallel Distributed Processing (PDP) group, a group of researchers who explored connectionist models of cognition. Their two-volume book, "Parallel Distributed Processing: Explorations in the Microstructure of Cognition," published in 1986, further popularized neural networks and backpropagation.

- **Impact:** The 1986 paper by Rumelhart, Hinton, and Williams had a profound impact on the field of machine learning. It revitalized the field of neural networks and led to a resurgence of research in the area. Backpropagation became the standard algorithm for training neural networks and remains so to this day.

Other Independent Discoveries:

- **Linnainmaa in Finland (1970):** Independently of Werbos, Seppo Linnainmaa described an algorithm that included backpropagation for calculating the total derivatives of nested differentiable functions in his 1970 master's thesis. He didn't relate this to neural networks, however.

- **Yann LeCun (Late 1980s):** Yann LeCun, while a postdoctoral fellow with Hinton, independently derived backpropagation and demonstrated its practical application to tasks like handwritten digit recognition. His work helped solidify the algorithm's importance in real-world applications.

Post-Backpropagation Era (Late 1980s - Present):

- **Refinements and Extensions:** Since its popularization, backpropagation has been refined and extended in various ways. Researchers have developed techniques to improve its efficiency, stability, and generalization performance.

- **Deep Learning Revolution:** Backpropagation is the engine behind the deep learning revolution. The ability to train deep neural networks with many layers, made possible by backpropagation and advances in computing power, has led to breakthroughs in areas such as image recognition, natural language processing, and game playing.

- **Automatic Differentiation:** Backpropagation is a special case of a more general technique called automatic differentiation (AD). AD is a set of techniques for automatically computing derivatives of functions defined by computer programs. Modern deep learning frameworks rely heavily on AD for efficient gradient calculations.

k-means algorithm

The k-means algorithm, a widely used clustering method for partitioning data into k distinct groups, has a history that spans several decades and involves contributions from multiple researchers across different fields. While often attributed to MacQueen, its origins can be traced back to earlier work in signal processing and data analysis.

Here's a breakdown of the key historical milestones:

Early Precursors (1950s):

- **Hugo Steinhaus (1957):** The Polish mathematician Hugo Steinhaus, in a 1957 paper, proposed an algorithm that can be considered a precursor to k-means. He addressed the problem of dividing a heterogeneous population into homogeneous groups to minimize within-group variance. While not explicitly the k-means algorithm as we know it today, it laid some of the groundwork for the concept of partitioning data based on distance to centroids.

- **Lloyd's Algorithm (1957, Published 1982):** Stuart P. Lloyd, while working at Bell Labs in 1957, proposed an algorithm for pulse-code modulation (PCM) that is essentially the standard k-means algorithm. However, his work was not published until 1982 in the journal *IEEE Transactions on*

Information Theory. This is often referred to as "Lloyd's algorithm" or the "Lloyd-Max algorithm" (due to its connection to quantization and Max's work). Lloyd's algorithm is iterative and proceeds by:

1. **Initialization:** Choosing initial cluster centers.

2. **Assignment:** Assigning each data point to the nearest cluster center.

3. **Update:** Recalculating the cluster centers as the mean of the points assigned to each cluster.

4. **Repeat:** Repeating steps 2 and 3 until convergence (when the cluster assignments no longer change or a maximum number of iterations is reached).

The Development of K-Means:

- **James MacQueen (1967):** The term "k-means" was first used by James MacQueen in his 1967 paper, "Some Methods for classification and Analysis of Multivariate Observations," presented at the Fifth Berkeley Symposium on Mathematical Statistics and Probability. He described an algorithm similar to Lloyd's but with a slight difference in how the cluster centers were updated. In MacQueen's version, the cluster centers were updated immediately after each point was reassigned, whereas in Lloyd's algorithm, the update happens after all points are assigned. Because of this paper, the algorithm is often attributed to MacQueen, but MacQueen himself never claimed to have invented the underlying algorithm.

- **Forgy's Method (1965):** Edward W. Forgy published a very similar algorithm in 1965 in the journal *Biometrics*. This is generally considered to be the same as Lloyd's algorithm.

Popularization and Refinements (1970s - Present):

- **Hartigan and Wong (1979):** A widely used and cited variant of the k-means algorithm was proposed by John A. Hartigan and Manchek A. Wong in 1979. Their algorithm refined the iterative process and provided heuristics for improving the efficiency and quality of the clustering.

- **Computational Efficiency:** As computers became more powerful, k-means gained popularity due to its relative simplicity and computational efficiency. It became a standard technique in data mining, pattern recognition, and machine learning.

- **Initialization Strategies:** Researchers have explored various strategies for initializing the cluster centers, as the initial choice can affect the final clustering results. One popular method is k-means++, which aims to choose initial centers that are well-spaced and improve the quality of the final clustering.

- **Determining the Optimal 'k':** A significant area of research has focused on methods for determining the optimal number of clusters (k). Techniques like the elbow method, silhouette analysis, and the gap statistic are commonly used to guide the choice of k.

- **Applications:** K-means has been applied to a vast array of applications, including:

  o **Image Segmentation:** Grouping pixels into regions with similar colors or textures.

  o **Customer Segmentation:** Dividing customers into groups with similar purchasing behavior or demographics.

  o **Document Clustering:** Grouping documents based on their content similarity.

  o **Anomaly Detection:** Identifying outliers or unusual data points that do not belong to any cluster.

  o **Data Compression:** Vector quantization using k-means can be used to compress data.

- **Variants and Extensions:** Numerous variants and extensions of k-means have been developed, including:

  o **Kernel k-means:** Using kernel functions to find non-linear clusters.

  o **Fuzzy c-means:** Allowing data points to belong to multiple clusters with varying degrees of membership.

  o **K-medoids:** Using actual data points as cluster centers (medoids) instead of means, making it more robust to outliers.

Apriori Algorithm

The Apriori algorithm, a foundational algorithm in data mining for discovering frequent itemsets and association rules in transactional databases, has a relatively short but impactful history. Here's a breakdown of its development:

Early Data Mining and Market Basket Analysis (Pre-1990s):

- **The Need for Pattern Discovery:** In the late 1980s and early 1990s, as businesses began to accumulate large amounts of transactional data (e.g., supermarket sales, customer purchase records), there was a growing interest in extracting useful knowledge and patterns from this data.

- **Market Basket Analysis:** One specific area of interest was market basket analysis, which aims to identify items that are frequently purchased together. This information can be used for various purposes, such as product placement, cross-selling, and targeted marketing.

- **Early Approaches:** Initial approaches to finding association rules were often based on exhaustive enumeration, which was computationally expensive and impractical for large databases with many items.

The Development of the Apriori Algorithm (1993-1994):

- **Rakesh Agrawal and Ramakrishnan Srikant at IBM Almaden (1993):** The Apriori algorithm was developed by Rakesh Agrawal and Ramakrishnan Srikant while working at the IBM Almaden Research Center. They first introduced the concept in their 1993 paper, "Fast Algorithms for Mining Association Rules in Large Databases," presented at the International Conference on Very Large Data Bases (VLDB).

- **The Apriori Principle:** The key innovation of the Apriori algorithm is its use of the "Apriori principle" to prune the search space efficiently. The principle states that:

  ○ "All nonempty subsets of a frequent itemset must also be frequent."

  ○ Conversely, "If an itemset is infrequent, then all its supersets must also be infrequent."

- **How Apriori Works:** The algorithm works iteratively:

1.   **Candidate Generation:** It starts by identifying frequent individual items (1-itemsets) in the database.

2.   **Pruning:** In each subsequent iteration, it generates candidate k-itemsets from the frequent (k-1)-itemsets found in the previous iteration. The Apriori principle is used to prune candidate itemsets that cannot be frequent based on the frequency of their subsets.

3.   **Support Counting:** It then scans the database to count the support (frequency) of the remaining candidate itemsets.

4.   **Frequent Itemset Selection:** Itemsets that meet the minimum support threshold are identified as frequent k-itemsets.

5. **Iteration:** Steps 2-4 are repeated until no more frequent itemsets are found.

- **Association Rule Generation:** Once frequent itemsets are identified, association rules can be generated from them. An association rule is of the form X => Y, where X and Y are disjoint itemsets. The rule's confidence is the conditional probability that a transaction contains Y given that it contains X.

- **Agrawal, Imieliński, and Swami (1993):** In another influential paper published in 1993, "Mining Association Rules between Sets of Items in Large Databases," Rakesh Agrawal, along with Tomasz Imieliński and Arun Swami, explored different algorithms for generating association rules from transactional databases.

Impact and Subsequent Developments (1994-Present):

- **Rapid Adoption:** The Apriori algorithm quickly became the standard algorithm for frequent itemset mining and association rule discovery. Its efficiency and relative simplicity made it a popular choice for analyzing large transactional databases.

- **Improvements and Variations:** Researchers have proposed various improvements and variations to the basic Apriori algorithm, including:

  o **Hash-Based Techniques:** Using hash tables to improve the efficiency of candidate generation and support counting.

- o **Partitioning:** Dividing the database into partitions that can be processed independently.

- o **Sampling:** Using sampling to estimate the support of itemsets, reducing the number of database scans required.

- o **FP-Growth (Frequent Pattern Growth):** An alternative algorithm that avoids candidate generation altogether by constructing a compact data structure called an FP-tree and extracting frequent itemsets directly from the tree.

- **Applications:** Apriori and its variants have been applied to a wide range of domains beyond market basket analysis, including:

- o **Web Usage Mining:** Discovering patterns in web server logs to understand user browsing behavior.

- o **Bioinformatics:** Analyzing gene expression data to identify genes that are frequently co-expressed.

- o **Intrusion Detection:** Identifying patterns in network traffic that may indicate malicious activity.

- o **Recommendation Systems:** Discovering items that are frequently purchased or viewed together to make recommendations to users.

- **Beyond Association Rules:** The principles of frequent itemset mining have been extended to other data mining tasks, such as sequential pattern mining, which aims to discover frequent sequences of events.

Apriori Algorithm

Glossary

Algorithm: A step-by-step procedure for solving a problem or performing a task, often implemented in software.

PageRank: An algorithm developed by Larry Page and Sergey Brin to rank web pages by their importance, based on the number and quality of backlinks.

RSA Algorithm: A cryptographic algorithm named after Rivest, Shamir, and Adleman. It uses public and private keys for secure data transmission.

Linear Programming: A mathematical optimization technique used to achieve the best outcome in a system modeled with linear relationships, subject to constraints.

Monte Carlo Algorithm: A method using random sampling to solve problems that might be deterministic in principle but are computationally complex.

Genetic Algorithm: An optimization algorithm inspired by the process of natural selection, involving mutation, crossover, and selection.

Fast Fourier Transform (FFT): An efficient algorithm to compute the Discrete Fourier Transform (DFT), widely used in signal processing.

Support Vector Machine (SVM): A supervised machine learning algorithm used for classification and regression by finding the optimal hyperplane.

Backpropagation: A key algorithm for training neural networks by propagating error gradients backward to update weights.

k-means Algorithm: An unsupervised machine learning algorithm for clustering data points into groups based on proximity to cluster centroids.

Apriori Algorithm: A popular algorithm used in data mining for finding frequent itemsets and deriving association rules.

Damping Factor: In PageRank, the probability of continuing to follow links rather than jumping randomly to another page.

Public-Key Cryptography: A cryptographic system using a pair of keys—one public and one private—for secure data transmission.

Hyperplane: A decision boundary in SVMs that separates data points into different classes.

Centroids: Points representing the center of clusters in k-means clustering.

Fitness Function: In genetic algorithms, a function that evaluates how close a solution is to the optimal solution.

Elbow Method: A technique for determining the optimal number of clusters in k-means clustering by analyzing the variance explained.

Overfitting: A situation where a model learns the training data too well, including noise, leading to poor performance on new data.

Vanishing Gradients: A challenge in deep learning where gradients become very small, making it hard for neural networks to learn.

Lift: A metric used in association rules to measure the strength of a rule compared to random chance.

Glossary

References

1. PageRank - Wikipedia, accessed December 28, 2024, https://en.wikipedia.org/wiki/PageRank

2. Page Rank – The History and Evolution of Google's Website Ranking Algorithm - Copymate, accessed December 28, 2024, https://copymate.app/blog/multi/page-rank-the-history-and-evolution-of-googles-website-ranking-algorithm/

3. PageRank Algorithm: How Does it Work and What is Its Impact on SEO?, accessed December 28, 2024, https://www.internallinkjuicer.com/hub/seo/pagerank/

4. Promise and Pitfalls of Extending Google's PageRank Algorithm to Citation Networks - PMC, accessed December 28, 2024, https://pmc.ncbi.nlm.nih.gov/articles/PMC6671494/

5. RSA (cryptosystem) - Wikipedia, accessed December 28, 2024, https://en.wikipedia.org/wiki/RSA_(cryptosystem)

6. www.veritas.com, accessed December 28, 2024, https://www.veritas.com/information-center/rsa-encryption#:~:text=It%20allows%20the%20encryption%20and,signature%20using%20a%20public%20key.

7. Linear programming - Wikipedia, accessed December 28, 2024, https://en.wikipedia.org/wiki/Linear_programming

8. Linear Programming: Definition, Formula, Examples, Problems - GeeksforGeeks, accessed December 28, 2024, https://www.geeksforgeeks.org/linear-programming/

9. corporatefinanceinstitute.com, accessed December 28, 2024, https://corporatefinanceinstitute.com/resources/career-map/sell-side/capital-markets/what-are-algorithms-algos/#:~:text=Algorithms%20are%20introduced%20to%20automate,timing%2C%20and%20other%20mathematical%20models.

10. 10 Algorithms that Have Changed the World | by Seattle Web Design, accessed December 28, 2024, https://webdesignseattle.medium.com/10-algorithms-that-have-changed-the-world-541ee82adcc6

References

11. What Is The Algorithmic Economy - Ian Khan "The Futurist" - CNN, BBC, Bloomberg Featured Keynote Speaker covering AI, Innovation, Leadership, accessed December 28, 2024, https://www.iankhan.com/what-is-the-algorithmic-economy/

12. Economic Implications of Algorithmic Trading, accessed December 28, 2024, https://gjle.in/2024/03/31/economic-implications-of-algorithmic-trading/

13. Monte Carlo method - Wikipedia, accessed December 28, 2024, https://en.wikipedia.org/wiki/Monte_Carlo_method

14. Monte Carlo Simulation: What It Is, How It Works, History, 4 Key Steps - Investopedia, accessed December 28, 2024, https://www.investopedia.com/terms/m/montecarlosimulation.asp

15. Monte Carlo simulations will change the way we treat patients with proton beams today - PMC, accessed December 28, 2024, https://pmc.ncbi.nlm.nih.gov/articles/PMC4112394/

16. How Medical Treatment Algorithms Are Shaping the Healthcare Industry - IRIS retinal screening, accessed December 28, 2024, https://retinalscreenings.com/blog/medical-treatment-algorithms/

17. Genetic algorithm - Wikipedia, accessed December 28, 2024, https://en.wikipedia.org/wiki/Genetic_algorithm

18. Genetic Algorithm Applications in Machine Learning - Turing, accessed December 28, 2024, https://www.turing.com/kb/genetic-algorithm-applications-in-ml

19. Genetic algorithms and deep learning strengths and limits - Lumenalta, accessed December 28, 2024, https://lumenalta.com/insights/genetic-algorithms

20. Fast Fourier transform - Wikipedia, accessed December 28, 2024, https://en.wikipedia.org/wiki/Fast_Fourier_transform

21. Fast Fourier Transform Explained | Built In, accessed December 28, 2024, https://builtin.com/articles/fast-fourier-transform

22. Support Vector Machine (SVM) Algorithm - GeeksforGeeks, accessed December 28, 2024, https://www.geeksforgeeks.org/support-vector-machine-algorithm/

23. Support vector machine in Machine Learning - GeeksforGeeks, accessed December 28, 2024, https://www.geeksforgeeks.org/support-vector-machine-in-machine-learning/

24. www.ibm.com, accessed December 28, 2024, https://www.ibm.com/think/topics/backpropagation#:~:text=Backpropagation%20is%20a%20machine%20learning,(AI)%20%E2%80%9Clearn.%E2%80%9D

25. Backpropagation - Wikipedia, accessed December 28, 2024, https://en.wikipedia.org/wiki/Backpropagation

26. K-means Clustering: Algorithm, Applications, Evaluation Methods, and Drawbacks, accessed December 28, 2024, https://towardsdatascience.com/k-means-clustering-algorithm-applications-evaluation-methods-and-drawbacks-aa03e644b48a

27. K-Means Clustering: Use Cases, Advantages and Working Principle - Bombay Softwares, accessed December 28, 2024, https://www.bombaysoftwares.com/blog/introduction-to-k-means-clustering

28. quickframe.com, accessed December 28, 2024, https://quickframe.com/blog/how-do-social-media-algorithms-work/#:~:text=What%20Are%20Social%20Media%20Algorithms,discover%E2%80%9D%20outside%20their%20own%20community.

29. What are the challenges with K-Means? - csias, accessed December 28, 2024, https://www.csias.in/what-are-the-challenges-with-k-means/

30. Unveiling the Impact of Social Media Algorithms: How They Shape Our Culture and Decision-Making | by Patrick OConnell | Reciprocal | Medium, accessed December 28, 2024, https://medium.com/reciprocall/unveiling-the-impact-of-social-media-algorithms-how-they-shape-our-culture-and-decision-making-a14eeb628229

31. Apriori Algorithm - GeeksforGeeks, accessed December 28, 2024, https://www.geeksforgeeks.org/apriori-algorithm/

32. Algorithms and Economic Justice: A Taxonomy of Harms and a Path Forward for the Federal Trade Commission - Yale Law School, accessed December 28, 2024, https://law.yale.edu/sites/default/files/area/center/isp/documents/algorithms_and_economic_justice_master_final.pdf

References

33. Ethics of Algorithms – Why Should We Care? | Kilian Vieth and Joanna Bronowicka - tbd, accessed December 28, 2024, https://www.tbd.community/en/a/ethics-algorithms-why-should-we-care

34. Ethical algorithm design should guide technology regulation - Brookings Institution, accessed December 28, 2024, https://www.brookings.edu/articles/ethical-algorithm-design-should-guide-technology-regulation/

Eugene Garfield. (2024, December 13). In *Wikipedia*. https://en.wikipedia.org/wiki/Eugene_Garfield

Jacob L. Moreno. (2024, December 19). In *Wikipedia*. https://en.wikipedia.org/wiki/Jacob_L._Moreno

Clifford Cocks. (2024, September 22). In Wikipedia. https://en.wikipedia.org/wiki/Clifford_Cocks

Joseph Fourier. (2024, December 2). In Wikipedia. https://en.wikipedia.org/wiki/Joseph_Fourier

Leonid Kantorovich. (2024, October 24). In Wikipedia. https://en.wikipedia.org/wiki/Leonid_Kantorovich

Wassily Leontief. (2024, December 27). In Wikipedia. https://en.wikipedia.org/wiki/Wassily_Leontief

John von Neumann. (2024, December 29). In Wikipedia. https://en.wikipedia.org/wiki/John_von_Neumann

Lord Kelvin. (2024, December 20). In Wikipedia. https://en.wikipedia.org/wiki/Lord_Kelvin

Enrico Fermi. (2024, December 25). In Wikipedia. https://en.wikipedia.org/wiki/Enrico_Fermi

Stanisław Ulam. (2024, December 4). In Wikipedia. https://en.wikipedia.org/wiki/Stanis%C5%82aw_Ulam

John Henry Holland. (2024, November 22). In Wikipedia. https://en.wikipedia.org/wiki/John_Henry_Holland

Carl Friedrich Gauss. (2024, December 27). In *Wikipedia.* https://en.wikipedia.org/wiki/Carl_Friedrich_Gauss

Hugo Steinhaus. (2024, November 21). In *Wikipedia.* https://en.wikipedia.org/wiki/Hugo_Steinhaus

References

More Books by the Author:

Critical Thinking is Your Superpower

Cultivating Critical Thinking in an AI-Driven World

Available on Amazon **(ISBN-13: 979-8303554634)**
https://www.amazon.com/dp/B0DQDN48MX

Beyond the Algorithm: An Attempt to Honor the Human Mind in the Age of Artificial Intelligence (Wittgenstein Reloaded)

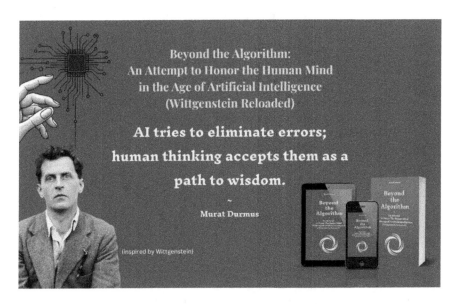

Available on Amazon **(ISBN-13: 979-8876790330)**
https://www.amazon.com/dp/B0CSWMMD39

The Cognitive Biases Compendium

Explore over 150 Cognitive Biases (with examples) to make better decisions, think critically, solve problems effectively, and communicate more accurately.

The Cognitive Biases Compendium

Explore over 150 Cognitive Biases (with examples) to make better decisions, think critically, solve problems effectively, and communicate more accurately.

"Bias here, Bias there;
Watch out,
Bias everywhere!"

"Let's learn more about our human biases to make less biased conclusions in the future."

Available on Amazon **(ISBN-13: 979-8851721496)**
https://www.amazon.com/dp/B0C9SF8KZW

MINDFUL AI

Reflections on Artificial Intelligence

Inspirational Thoughts & Quotes on Artificial Intelligence
(Including 13 illustrations, articles & essays for the fundamental understanding of AI)

The field of AI is highly interdisciplinary & evolutionary. The more AI penetrates our life and environment, the more comprehensive the points we have to consider and adapt. Technological developments are far ahead of ethical & philosophical interpretations; this fact is disturbing.

We need to close this gap as soon as possible.

~ (Mindful AI)

Available on Amazon:
https://www.amazon.com/dp/B0BKMK6HLJ

Kindle: **(ASIN: B0BKLCKM22)**
Paperback: **(ISBN-13: 979-8360396796)–**

INSIDE ALAN TURING: QUOTES & CONTEMPLATIONS

Alan Turing is generally considered the father of computer science and artificial intelligence. He was also a theoretical biologist who developed algorithms to explain complex patterns using simple inputs and random fluctuation as a side hobby. Unfortunately, his life tragically ended in suicide in 1954, after he was chemically castrated as punishment (instead of prison) for 'criminal' gay acts.

"We can only see a short distance ahead, but we can see plenty there that needs to be done."

~ Alan Turing

Available on Amazon:
https://www.amazon.com/dp/B09K25RTQ6

Kindle: **(ASIN: B09K3669BX)**
Paperback: **(ISBN- 979-8751495848)**